Keep Calm, It's Just a Brain Tumor

My Year of Wabi-Sabi Healing

Keep Calm, It's Just a Brain Tumor

My Year of Wabi-Sabi Healing

Susan Spector

ISBN: 978-0991086177

KEEP CALM, IT'S JUST A BRAIN TUMOR

Dream List Books

An Imprint of Bellastoria Press

P.O. Box 60341, Longmeadow, MA 01116

Cover drawing by Printee Line Drawings

Drawing of Dorothy and Alice by Helen Green

https://helengreenillustration.com/

For Cameron,

who carries me through the storm and teaches me the

meaning of the word devotion

"There is no more serious diagnosis in all human beings than a brain tumor because it not only is a medical issue that has to be treated, but it actually affects the psyche, the soul of the entire personhood of a human being."

– Dr. Steven Kalkanis, Chair of Neurosurgery
Henry Ford Health Systems and Cancer Institute
Detroit, Michigan

Table of Contents

Author's Note

This is a work of creative nonfiction. It reflects my own recollections of experiences over time and interpretation of conversations and experiences that took place. In many cases, I could not remember exact words said by people or events due to cognitive deficits, a wacky mind and a flawed and imperfect memory from brain trauma. I had to fill in the gaps as best I could. The events are portrayed to the best of my memory. Some names and identifying details have been changed to protect the privacy of some of those involved. Opinions, as well as errors, are my own.

Rabbi Naomi Levy tells a famous tale in her book, Einstein and the Rabbi:

"Once a great Hasidic rabbi was dying. His disciples crowded around him and the rabbi began to weep. His disciples said to him, "Rebbe, why are you crying?" The rabbi replied, "My whole life is passing before me and I suddenly see that I had it all wrong. I was mistaken. The moments in my life that I thought were extraordinary were actually quite ordinary. And the moments that I thought were ordinary were the most luminous of all. I wish I had understood this!"

PART I

Wake-Up Call

CHAPTER 1: AWAKENING BY MY NEUROSURGEONS

"Waking up to who you are requires letting go of who you imagine yourself to be."
– Alan Watts

Sounds of the room carry through the air before I am truly awake. I hear talking, footsteps shuffling across the linoleum floor, doors opening and closing, monitors beeping and machines humming. The last thing I remember is closing my eyes. I was told to go to my happy place, but that's not me. I tried to visualize a warm tropical beach or a fiery ocean sunset, but I am a worrier by nature and couldn't do it.

My last thoughts before closing my eyes were worries about the sidewalls of our large litter box getting cleaned properly. Our cat Rom does not have the best toilet etiquette and sometimes he is too lazy to squat, so we have an oversize box that catches his urine on the sidewalls when he pees while standing up. I am the one who notices it and wipes it down. Who thinks about these things before going under anesthesia?

Brain surgery is unlike any other surgery. Other kinds of operations have you wondering and hoping you're going to wake up. This kind has you worry that you might not be there when you do wake up. Pre-surgery cat box concerns remain part of our family lore.

I don't remember having dreams or recall being asleep. I hear someone calling my name. Wait, so I can hear. Thank you. This sounds like a wake-up call. I open my eyes. I haven't yet put it together that I had brain surgery, but I know that things are changed. Things are blurry, but I can see. Thank you. I know something happened to the top of my head. I am groggy and confused. I'm scared and nauseous, yet I am also feeling grateful and lucky to be alive. I am chilly.

My throat hurts and I am thirsty. Both my wrists burn and I see coils of plastic tubing dangling from the veins in my forearm and wrists, slightly red in color from blood in the line. I think there is another coil of plastic tubing under my gown, in my groin area.

I wonder if that is a catheter so I don't have to leave the bed to pee. This is good, I can think. Thank you. My head is too heavy to lift off the slightly raised pillow. I try sitting up, but can't. They tell me to lie back down. In another day, they will tell me to sit up and move when I just want to lie down.

I can hear my own hoarse voice, my speech slurred. "What time is it?" I ask of no one in particular. I ask the same question again to whoever happens to be in the room.

"What time is it? What time is it?"

Later, I will think about when I slipped the stretchy Timex watch off my mother's tiny wrist, about a half hour after she was pronounced dead. I always wondered why she felt the need to know the time while lying in a hospice bed, waiting to die.

Through a haze, I see the kind, smiling face of a beatific Indian man. I know this is good. He is a blurry image, but soon starts to swim into focus through my tears. I am weeping, but I can see. Thank you. He stands over my bed, looking down at me with a peaceful expression. I'm not sure if his hands are folded in prayer pose. If not, they should have been.

I hear him thanking me. This is also good, I can hear. Why is HE thanking ME? I somehow know this man just saved my life. I can think, but I'm confused. This isn't right. It should be the other way around. I should be thanking him. I want to express the profound gratitude I feel all over my body, but now my weeping has turned to crying and I can't speak. I can only cry. Thank you.

My body is not cooperating with my groggy mind. I am sobbing uncontrollably. I am not feeling any pain. Maybe all these tears are what is called a "good cry remedy." All I feel is a grateful sense of well-being. Intuitively and through my soul, I know I am forever changed. I will not be the same person and life will never again be the same. I believe I will be forever grateful. This awakening experience will teach me how to live more fully. I will learn more about this later.

Suddenly I feel like I'm going to be sick and my stomach begins to heave. The smell of disinfectant fills my nostrils. I turn my head. The man reaches out and hands me a blue plastic cone-shaped bag. I turn, hold it over my mouth and vomit. Hardly anything comes up.

This beautiful man is a vision. And he is real. I turn back to look at him. My sobbing has turned back to weeping. I am feeling better after vomiting. My mind slowly starts putting things together. I recognize this man.

I can sort of remember he is one of my brilliant neurosurgeons. I can't remember his name.

He comes to visit me the next day. My face lights up with a wide smile when I see him standing in my hospital room doorway. He stands there for a minute, waiting to be invited into my recovery room. He smiles and his hand makes a knock-knock motion in the air, waiting for me to invite him in. The day before, that same hand entered into the deep recesses of my brain needing no permission to enter. He steps inside the room and stands by the side of the bed, looking down on me, benevolently.

"It is good to see you. Do you have any questions?"

"I hear a loud sloshing noise when I move my head from side to side. Is that the sound of water on the brain?"

"No, obstructive hydrocephalus was resolved with surgery," he explains in a matter of fact medical way.

"Swooshing sound is from a small air bubble called pneumocephalus left behind after the procedure."

With confidence and a calming voice, he assures me, "'twill resolve."

The word resolve is often used in technical neurosurgical terms, but for me it will become a spiritual lesson and a metaphor. Everything eventually resolves because nothing is permanent. In that moment, this man who helped save my life is renamed and will forever be known by me and my family as Dr. Devi 'Twill-resolve.

Dr. Bendok, Chief of Neurosurgery, The Boss, Bernie, also stops by for a brief visit on morning rounds. He sits down on the end of my bed.

"How are you feeling?"

Nauseous, exhausted, blurry vision and a killer headache, my answer came out snarky,

"I don't know, is crap a feeling?"

So much for my big plan of "eternal and infinite" gratitude. It lasted about twenty-four hours. Dr. Bendok points his finger at me. He uses his index finger in the same way a Zen master uses his flat wooden pointer sticks, designed to gently strike sleepy meditators to wake up their concentration. Pointing, he gets all up in my face and says,

"You couldn't walk when I met you. You're better!"

He stands up and walks out of the room.

BOOM. Mic drop.

And so begins my new normal, my life metaphor of waking up from brain surgery. There is nothing warm, fuzzy or comforting in Dr. Bendok's reminder, but it is an enduring and powerful lesson. Whenever I am tempted to kvetch or complain about something small, like stiff joints, arthritis aches and pains or fatigue, I remember this Zen master's wisdom. I point my index finger and remind myself, "You're better. Wake up. Do better."

The endoscopic third ventriculostomy (ETV) surgical procedure was successful in treating my obstructive hydrocephalus. "Water on the brain" is the colloquial term for it and to say this ETV procedure was life-changing is an understatement.

The Hydrocephalus Association estimates around 20% of people with this condition are often misdiagnosed with Alzheimer's or Parkinson's. The main symptoms are dementia, incontinence and a shuffling gait, and present the same for all three diseases.

My condition of obstructive hydrocephalus was caused by cerebral spinal fluid filling up the spaces within my brain and then enlarging them. There is only a limited amount of space in our skulls, so this can be a deadly condition if left untreated. The enlarged brain spaces, called ventricles, look like butterfly wings when I am later shown images of them on a large computer monitor.

I got incredibly lucky. After getting dropped into this place of primal fear with loss of control of body and mind, my brilliant neurosurgeons reversed my symptoms 100% through their skill, knowledge and courage. I often wonder how many less fortunate people diagnosed with Parkinson's disease might be suffering from hydrocephalus and could possibly be treated with an ETV or a shunt? The same goes for Alzheimer's. The symptoms of these heartbreaking diseases mirror those of hydrocephalus conditions. The only difference between people suffering from Parkinson's, dementia and me is that I got cured. I had a miracle diagnosis and a bigger miraculous medical treatment. It is still really hard for me to wrap my mind around this.

But my journey doesn't end with my miracle surgery. The surgical procedure left behind an inoperable tumor in the middle of my brain, in the pineal gland. The angle of approach was too steep and dangerous to reach for a biopsy during the ETV procedure and my neurosurgeons exercised great restraint in not forcing through to reach it. The tumor was placed on a Watch and Wait (WaWa) treatment plan. The watching would be done through regular MRI brain scans. The waiting would be done by me figuring out how to best manage the anxiety and uncertainties of living with a brain tumor. Later, I would also realize that I had a second smaller brain tumor, but had temporarily denied its existence, since the doctors expressed virtually no concern over it.

Over time and a lot of processing, writing and thinking, the WaWa medical treatment plan will morph into my day-to-day life philosophy and spiritual practice.

CHAPTER 2: EXPLORING FRAGILITY AND RESILIENCE THROUGH KINTSUGI

"Our bodies prime our metaphors,
and our metaphors prime how we think and act."
– James Geary

S ometimes called golden joinery, Kintsugi is an ancient Japanese way of repairing broken pottery by mending areas of the breakage with golden lacquer. It treats the breakage and repair as part of the history of the broken object, rather than a flaw to disguise. The technique draws attention to and celebrates the imperfections of the broken vessels. I don't know it yet, but I emerged from brain surgery, fully transformed, just like a repaired Kintsugi pottery bowl.

Dr. Bendok, aka Dr. Kintsugi, made a perforation in my precious and sacred material. Instead of repairing a crack, he had to burst through my third ventricle to make one. Songwriter and artist Leonard Cohen says, *"There's a crack, a crack in everything, that's how the light gets in."* In my case, that's how the cerebral spinal fluid flows freely. It too is a celebration of imperfect perfection, of letting the light in.

I met another Kintsugi artist when I had my first hair appointment, three months after surgery. This artist took my original Kintsugi work and drew a new piece of head art on the surface of the canvas. This second artist's name is Ginny and she is my kind, talented and humble hairdresser.

I don't know what kind of golden epoxy Dr. Kintsugi used, but it took Ginny close to an hour to painstakingly coax the excess out with a thin comb normally used for teasing hair. She found a few dreadlock-like strands of hair that had been glued onto my shaved bald spot. I ask Ginny if she thought that hair would grow back. She looked doubtful but said nothing. This will become a permanent bald spot in the curious shape of a horseshoe.

Once she removed the dreadlock-like strands that resembled hair extensions, I realized they were made out of my own frizzy hair and had been shaved off so the original Kintsugi artist could work on a clean canvas. Once Ginny removed them, she put a stop to the ridiculous comb-over cover up that gave me the illusion to think my scars were not showing.

Ginny was like a detective, finding all kinds of weird things on my head. She worked with patience and a complete lack of judgment. I had been nervous to sit in her chair. A friend had given me a gift certificate for Ginny's home-based hair services. She lives in our neighborhood and I could walk to the appointment, which was great because I wasn't yet cleared or ready to drive. Ginny assured me she knew exactly what to do and would be very gentle. I think I brought a bottle of baby shampoo with me, following the recommendations in my post-op shampoo instructions.

She surveyed the lumps, grooves and bumps on my head. She seemed a little surprised when I showed her the smooth dome that pops slightly out of the top of my scalp. It's the dome of my Ommaya reservoir, a medical device Dr. Kintsugi implanted in my third ventricle as an insurance policy during surgery. It will serve as easy brain access if I ever need cerebral spinal fluid pumped out or medicine pumped in at some point in the future. It sits at the base of my forever bald spot that will never grow hair again. Ginny only showed curiosity and interest, no sign of queasiness. Thank you, Ginny.

As she patiently worked her magic, she came upon another mystery at the bald excavation site. There was a handful of multi-colored shiny glitter, stuck to the surgical epoxy, sparkling in the light. I had no idea where it came from.

Later, my friend Greg made a confession. He was visiting my boyfriend Cameron and me and we were strolling the main street of Old Towne, Cottonwood after a lovely lunch outing. We popped in for a visit to an odd shop that specializes in craft supplies for glitter art projects. None of us are crafters, but a strange "life-size" unicorn made out of glitter lured Greg and me into the odd shop. Greg secretly sprinkled a handful of glitter on the top of my head as a prank during our visit as Cameron sat outside on a bench, happy to people watch and wait for us. Cameron has no interest in glitter art.

Greg assumed I would find the glitter soon after he anointed me and we would have a laugh together. Little did he know, the surgical epoxy on the top of my head hadn't fully cured yet, so the glitter stuck to my head canvas. My beautiful new scars got an extra special shiny sparkle effect sprinkled on the top. Greg too was celebrating the flaws of the scars and adding to it with a handful of confetti glitter. We are still having a laugh.

When Greg read this vignette, he said there was one correction I needed to make. It wasn't a prank; it was a blessing. I have more blessings in my life than I deserve. Thank you, Greg.

Today we find ourselves in the middle of a pandemic and diligently practicing social isolation. I am sporting an uncut wild mane, along with matching pandemic eyebrows. I look forward to seeing my artists and friends when, one day, we can hopefully get this damn virus under control.

CHAPTER 3: WABI-SABI HEALING

"It is not impermanence that makes us suffer. What makes us suffer is wanting things to be permanent, when they are not."
– Thich Nhat Hanh

I open my eyes, stretch, reach down and give my companion pointer dog Paisley's black and white head a stroking. She groans with pleasure, but doesn't lift her head. My boyfriend Cameron is sleeping next to me, his breath steady and eyes fluttering with dreams. I yawn, and silently mouth the Hebrew words of my short Jewish morning prayer, expressing gratitude for waking up, before getting out of bed. *Modeh Ani...*

I had gotten up to pee a few hours before, so I didn't need to rush out of bed. I reach out, grab my fully charged Kindle and open Yahoo mail. I do a quick scan to see if anything looks interesting. Before the global pandemic hit, this mailbox contained traditional communications; blogs, newsletters and messages from friends. Today there are Zoom invitation links for a bar mitzvah, a bris (only an

Orthodox rabbi could organize this invite), my memoir
writing group and weekly book club.

I notice a new *Buddhist Boot Camp* blog by Timber
Hawkeye. I select it to read, even though it is far down the
list of unopened messages. Timber is an Israeli man living
in the US, spreading Buddhist wisdom in easy-to-read
plain language. I first discovered him in my carefree early
retirement days of leisure reading.

The blog topic this month is wabi-sabi. Never heard of
it and wondered if it was a Japanese food, maybe some kind
of sushi dish. I remembered feeling ill once from eating too
many hot wabi-sabi flavored spiced peanuts on a road trip
in the Florida Keys. I didn't think Timber would be writing
about food, unless it was about how to eat mindfully.

As I read, I learn wabi-sabi derives from Buddhist
teachings and ancient Japanese philosophical ideals that
places value on the beauty of imperfection. It is a life
perspective centered around the celebration of flawed
beauty and the acceptance of impermanence and natural
cycles of growth and decay.

I begin to think about the imperfections in my brain
and start connecting the dots. Was my imperfect brain a

thing of beauty? Then I thought, here I go again, obsessed with these tumors, I tend to view everything through their prism. I think about an arranged marriage between this wabi-sabi philosophy and my flawed and tumored brain.

I finish the blog, roll out of bed and head for the kitchen. I grab the 32-ounce green plastic bottle and pour my ritual first-thing-in-the-morning celery juice. Last summer, three months after my emergency brain surgery, we followed doctor's orders and took a vacation to heal. We stopped in Victor, Idaho on our way to Montana. While doing laundry in the RV park laundromat, I struck up a conversation with a random fellow camper who insisted green celery elixir prevented and possibly cured cancer.

"It's something that Big Pharma doesn't want you to know about."

I don't have cancer, but I do have two lumps of rogue silly cells camping out in my brain that have remained stable through every scan of the past year. This is the same amount of time I've been drinking the green elixir, ever since having this fateful conversation. Superstition or magic, it's one of my daily rituals.

I quietly return to bed with my green juice magic. Cameron and Paisley are still sleeping, snoring in harmony. I bring the Kindle back to life and reread Timber's blog, twice. With each repetition, the wabi-sabi concept resonates on deeper levels. I am beginning to feel a glimmer of something exciting brewing in my mind. I need to know more. I fire up the Silk browser and type wabi-sabi into the search bar.

It is a Japanese aesthetic and a way of living. In addition to the focus on finding beauty in the imperfections of life, it places value on the natural states of decay. Sounds like Kintsugi art and my brain tumors. It's about gratefully accepting the uncertainty and impermanence of all things in this world. Bingo. I intuitively know if I could develop a practice around this philosophy, then it could be a useful method to cope with my brain tumors, the gurus I have named Pinena and L'il Miss Pollyanna. You will meet these spiritual teachers a little later.

Paisley and I head out for our morning walkies. She does her usual lizard chasing and searching out smelly things to roll on. I need quiet time to think. I do my best thinking out in nature and today my thoughts are focused on wabi-sabi. I notice connections to this newly discovered wisdom of impermanence while walking in the natural high desert terrain. I smell dried up and decayed yellow grass, flattened in the heat and turned to hay. Wabi-sabi. I notice the agave stalks that have turned from green to red, having bloomed and are now getting ready to die after their once-in-a-lifetime flowering. I've heard it supposedly takes them a century to bloom, and then they die. Wabi-sabi, the natural order. Everything changes. Everything is impermanent. Nothing lasts. Nothing is finished. Everything out here in the desert is perfect by nature of its growth, decay and imperfection.

I start to see the potential for wabi-sabifying my tumors, the lumps that make my brain imperfect. These rogue cells may grow, decay, shrink or even disappear. Their current stable state can, like life, change at any time. Only two things are certain about them. They won't always be as they are now. And they are a gift.

CHAPTER 4: PINENA AND POLLYANNA

Part 1: Pinena and the Rabbi

Yom Kippur 2019

It happened at a Yom Kippur Jewish high holiday service in a conference room and makeshift shul in the Marriott Hotel in Sedona, Arizona. The congregation is small and without a physical place for prayer yet. The Orthodox Chabad rabbi rents the hotel space for the high holidays. For me, this is perfect space for my Jewish ritual and ceremony.

Before the services begin, I sit in the hotel lobby, sipping a glass of house merlot. This may be my last glass of wine, as I realize that alcohol no longer tastes good after brain surgery. It might be what they call acute sensitivity, a common post-op trait that can make you super sensitive to noise, sounds, and all kinds of different stimuli in the environment. My sensitivity happens to be alcohol, so I don't drink any more. Maybe it is simply not wanting to ingest anything that will mess with my brain chemistry or affect my ability to think, keep my balance or function. It feels disrespectful to my incredibly resilient brain that has done me a solid by bouncing back so well and recovering from its wet, wobbly and wacky nightmare.

A nightly ritual disappears. I am glad it is alcohol and not caffeine. I wouldn't give up my morning coffee so easily. I've probably reached my lifetime quota for nightly glasses of merlot by now anyway.

The following Yom Kippur, 2020, we will be on an RV road trip, equipped with a DIY High Holidays in a Box. The box is filled with honey and apples to taste the sweetness of a new year and guidance on making my prayers and holiday a meaningful and inspiring experience, in the safety of our Covid-19-free motor home.

Cameron returns from the RV park store, gloved and masked, holding up a 3-pack of mini RumChata bottles. It reminds me of a friend I had to navigate a difficult separation from during the height of the Pinena adventure. I think about Yom Kippur forgiveness. The familiar gold-topped white pearlized plastic containers always remind me of pretty perfume bottles. It brought back memories of boozy house parties with our neighbors where I was first introduced to this delicious creamy liquor made with real Horchata and blended with Caribbean rum. It's an authentic replica of the best Horchata I have ever tasted, made from rice, sugar, cinnamon and vanilla, with a hint of clove and cardamom.

Cameron asked me to share a toast. At first, I hesitated, but then remembered my new drinking ritual, which is to enjoy one annual toast during the Rosh Hashanah and Yom Kippur high holidays. We split the 100-milliliter mini bottle and it tasted pretty delicious. I had absolutely no desire for any more than that. Thank you, new brain.

Before the brain maelstrom, I only had a vague awareness of how easily my one glass of merlot could slip into two or three and just how slippery of a slope I was on. Thank you, Pinena. Fortunately, my new brain serves as a reminder, by disappearing my taste for alcohol.

I see the Rabbi crossing the lobby, loaded up with prayer books in one arm and four of his young children in tow behind him. They are all dressed up in dark suits and crisp white dress shirts. The boys and the Rabbi are wearing their tallit, the prayer shawls with the tzitzit tassels hanging down like shirttails. Tzitzit are specially knotted ritual fringes attached to the bottom of the prayer shawl and worn by observant, Jewish Orthodox males. Their heads are covered in silky black yarmulkes, or skullcaps, and they have matching silky purple ties. The little girl is wearing a frilly dress, lacy ankle socks and shiny, patent-leather MaryJane shoes.

I greet the Rabbi with a joyful Mazel Tov! His lovely wife just had a baby at 4:00 this very morning. I ask him how he is managing it all, conducting High Holiday services, a newborn and four young children in tow. The children are usually tended to by his wife. He smiles widely and just points his finger up towards the ceiling. I nod and return the smile.

I sit quietly in the conference room/makeshift synagogue, listening to the beautiful and soulful prayer melodies being sung out on this special night by the hazzan, the Hasidic cantor. My mind starts to wander and I start thinking about the Rabbi's plans for their new baby's naming ceremony. Suddenly, I am struck with an unexplained energy. This is Sedona, and we're close to a famous vortex energy, but I don't really believe in that stuff.

The mysterious energy speaks to me about a name for the head lodger lying deep inside my pineal gland, in the middle of my brain. This somber energy lets me know her name will be Pinena. Naming tumors is a common thing done in the brain tumor community. I'd always believed it was silly, something I never thought I would do.

Pinena. I have no idea where this came from. I am not up on my old testament stories and thought maybe she was a biblical character. I made a mental note to Google the name when I got home.

Yom Kippur, the highest holiday of the year for Jews, has a sheer magnetic force to it. It makes perfect sense to experience this energy tonight. It is powerful and has a sacred feel. I am starting to understand the gravity of the experience of my brain tumor that caused potentially deadly obstructive hydrocephalus. The whole point of the Yom Kippur holiday is its gravity. I begin to sense something has shifted. Something feels very different when the Yom Kippur prayers are over than it did when the service began.

Naming Pinena seems to take a lot of the fear away from her. By personifying her, she is somehow a friendlier entity. Maybe we could even have a conversation someday. As I travel the road of life's uncertainties, it becomes clearer that I should have conversations with my head lodger,

Pinena. I may find out why she is here, what she wants and if there is something I can do to help her disappear. At least I know the conversation wouldn't upset her the way it does other people. She is me.

I am making progress in the stages of grief around this illness, moving into acceptance, the fifth stage. Acceptance, patience and tolerance are the qualities I need and want to develop with this spiritual growth. I have an inoperable brain tumor that gives me an abundance of opportunities to develop these qualities. It is time to move on to making room for my new guest to settle peacefully into my head space. Listening to the hazzan's chanting as the background soundtrack, I intuitively recognize this time as a soul transformation. I suddenly want to give thanks for all Pinena has given me, even though I am terrified of her at the same time.

I've been invited to several baby naming ceremonies over the past year by my Chabad rabbis. They take the "be fruitful and multiply" commandment seriously. I've heard it said that procreation in the Hasidic community is a guarantee the Jewish religion will continue to thrive and I think there is some truth in that.

In traditional Jewish baby naming ceremonies, gratitude to G-d is always given first. Next, announcements will mention hearts overflowing with joy. I can get behind the gratitude for Pinena. As for the overflowing joy of the tumor presence in my world, nah... not so much.

Pinena's naming ceremony during this year's Yom Kipper services is like a Russian nesting doll, a ceremony inside a ceremony. I leave the sacred services a different person. Just like I woke up a different person after experiencing Bernie's sacred work in my emergency brain surgery. More emerging gratitude.

When I got home and Googled Pinena, I found her to be a somewhat minor biblical character who lives in the shadow of another woman, Hannah, the childless wife of Elkanah. After not producing children during ten years of marriage, Hannah and Elkanah believe she is barren, so he takes on Pinena as a second wife, a surrogate to fulfill the biblical mandate to be fruitful and multiply. Pinena births many sons and daughters.

One day, Hannah miraculously conceives and then Pinena disappears from the story. Hmm...I am well beyond the baby-making years, so I wonder what I must conceive or birth for Pinena to disappear from my story. Perhaps it will be this memoir.

I decide to treat my newly named head lodger Pinena like one of the guests in the famous poem, *The Guest House,* by the Sufi mystic, Rumi.

> "...Every morning a new arrival. A joy, a depression, a meanness. Some momentary awareness comes, an unexpected visitor. Welcome and entertain them all. Even if they're a crowd of sorrows who violently sweep your house of its furniture. Still treat each guest honorably. It may be clearing you out for some new delight...."

Along with a name, I endow Pinena with her own tag line wisdom reminder, "Life can turn on a dime."

That was the gift she brought to me when we were first introduced at that fateful meeting in the Neurosurgery wing inside the basement offices of the Mayo Clinic. As usual, I didn't recognize the gift or the wisdom at first.

Pinena is welcome to live in my shadow, like the biblical Pinena lived in Hannah's. But we are going to need to lay down a few roommate guidelines before we can all settle down and relax. As long as she doesn't cause any more expensive plumbing backups and I don't have to call in the elite and daring plumbing/engineering/neurosurgeon team of one, Dr. Kintsugi, to swoop back in for another rescue, then we're good. As long as she agrees not to demand more space, move furniture around or invite friends or relatives in for a visit, then she is welcome to live, grow old and continue to calcify in my/her quiet and remote deep brain sanctuary.

Fast forward a year. So far so good. Pinena is behaving and we are living harmoniously, in our symbiotic relationship.

Part 2: A Conversation with Pinena

Symbiotic *(adjective):*
- *involving interaction between two different organisms living in close physical association.*
- *denotes a mutually beneficial relationship between different people or groups.*

Recently I worked up the courage to engage in dialogue with Pinena.

Me: Pinena, where are you in the story? I mean I know you dwell inside the tiny pinecone shaped endocrine gland nestled between my left and right hemisphere, dead center and deep as you can go, inside my brain. I am not sure if you are living inside pineal gland territory proper, or do you live in an attached township, just outside of the gland's city limits? I have so many more questions, like what role do you want to play and how much do you want to say in the story?

Pinena: Hmm, I'd have to give that some thought, but glad you're asking. I don't like the way you expect me to be an all-knowing, all-intuitive third-eye source of wisdom. The way you sometimes think of my home, your pineal gland, as the stuff of myth, magic and legend, puts a lot of pressure on me. I've even heard you think (yes, I can hear you think) of it as the portal between physical and metaphysical dimensions and the gateway to your soul. I noticed you recently read about wisdom traditions that believe the pineal gland releases important biochemicals such as DMT, also known as the spirit molecule, a catalyst for intuition. Okay, I know we are living just outside of Sedona now, but geez, that's a lot of woo-woo.

I prefer the explanation Noreen gave you when she dropped off that old and yellowed children's pediatric patient brochure, *Learning About Tumors*. Maybe the preschool explanation is right. I'm just a lump of silly cells who don't work quite right, things got out of control and I grew bigger than you wanted me to grow. Oh, and I am sorry I made you feel unwell.

Me: Can you serve as my watch and wait Zen koan?

Pinena: What's a Zen koan?

Me: It is a paradoxical riddle primarily used in Zen Buddhism as a meditation training. It is usually a small phrase, just like 'watch and wait,' that challenges conventional thinking. The Zen masters said koans change how you live in the world by provoking insight. They can reveal truths about ourselves and the world. Simply put, they can show us the way to live.

Pinena: There you go again with the spiritual wisdom pressure. Let's just slow things down. Let's literally watch and wait. One thing I think we will need to figure out is how to best pair up living a wabi-sabi lifestyle while being on a watch and wait treatment protocol. Otherwise, I can see you getting too attached to staying on this plan forever. And we know deep down, nothing is forever.

Me: While we're at it, we should probably do a whole writing riff on attachments. Like how you are literally attached to me. And I am attached to making meaning out of you. We're symbiotic. Like the bumblebee and the flowering plant. The decorator crab and sea sponge. Like the intestinal bacteria that lives in our gut. The lichen's algae or fungus. The buffalo and the oxpecker. Or when a small fish cleans the teeth of a large fish and the large fish protects the small fish from predators. Or when an aging woman chooses a watch and wait treatment plan to protect her brain tumors from the sharp destruction of a surgeon's scalpel.

You know, the Buddha says the root of all suffering is attachment. It is an Orthodox Jewish teaching to never make plans, appointments or speak of future events without adding the words, G-d willing. This is said without fear, but rather as a simple reminder of the nature of things and impermanence. It is a reminder to hold things loosely, and not be too attached to outcomes, whether it's a lunch date with a friend or even a brain tumor MRI report.

Pinena: We are both very attached to resisting any more brain surgery. I know how much you love him, but I'm terrified of Bernie. I think he wants to come for my crown. He missed me last time. I eluded him by making his path too dangerous. And by the way, I do appreciate you protecting us by choosing and then speaking up for the watch and wait plan. Maybe I helped you out a bit and activated your power of intuition on that one. Slow things down. It was the right decision. I haven't grown in a year. Why make such an aggressive and invasive move just to get a piece of me? What's the rush? I'm not going anywhere. You know where to find me.

Me: That's really what it's all about, isn't it? Slowing things down. Seems to be a recurring theme on a few different planes. Slow down writing scenes. Slow down the decision about selling the Prescott house. Slow it all down. Watch and wait. I've read somewhere that Franz Kafka is said to have had a sign posted by his writing area that reads, simply, Wait. If it is good enough for Kafka grappling with writing about problems of existentialism in the face of an absurd universe, then it is good enough for me. And I am having this Watch and Wait conversation with you, Pinena, my primary brain tumor.

After Pinena's naming ceremony, I sit quietly in the makeshift shul, listening to the beautiful and soulful prayer melodies being sung out on this special night by the Hasidic cantor and leading the congregation in songful prayers. The settings are different, but the Hebrew melodies and sounds are familiar ones from my childhood.

I am seated behind two women who are dressed in fancy white dresses and chatting up a storm. Did they just attend Pinena's naming ceremony? Could they hear me chatting with Pinena, I wonder? I want them to be quiet now, but I can't even give them a side eye because they are in front of me, oblivious to my annoyance. The Rabbi stands in front of the ark, wearing his usual broad smile filled with his Hasidic joy. It is his natural disposition. He can obviously see and maybe even hear the muffled chatting of the ladies in front of me, but doesn't seem bothered by it. I wish he would just shush them.

Well, if it's not annoying him, then I should be okay with the chatting too, I think to myself. If I want to learn how to find calm and inner peace, who better to study than this happy Hasidic rabbi?

I decide to focus my attention on the hand-carved wooden portable Torah ark, big enough to hold just one scroll. The doors are shaped in a tree of life design. This ark is different from the one in the Chabad House in Prescott. The Prescott ark, where I used to attend services when I lived in my own house, is made from a repurposed gun cabinet. It was found at a local thrift shop and refinished by a right-wing gun enthusiast congregant named Gary. This always struck me as somehow wrong, but this is the wild west and now I can view it as wabi-sabi, imperfectly perfect. The cabinet's original purpose as a gun holder mixes too much violence with the sacred for me. But that's the reality of the world we live in. At least I am sure our sacred writings are positioned on the wall pointing in the direction of Jerusalem and what was that uncharacteristic remark President Obama made about people clinging to their guns and religion. And here I sit.

In Orthodox tradition, the men and women sit separately during prayer. Men were seated on the other side of the hotel room tonight, separated by a portable wooden partition. The top half of the partition was a laser cut decorative panel, allowing just enough visibility to see through to the other side. I peek through, trying to do so discreetly. I see there are more men than women here tonight. I don't see or hear any chatting going on the men's prayer side, just davening, the ritual recitation of prescribed prayers in the Jewish liturgy.

Part 3: Li'l Miss Pollyanna
Just a Little Schwannoma

"And though she be but little, she is fierce."
– Shakespeare, *A Midsummer Night's Dream*

I almost didn't name you. You were described in medical terms as a "stable little 8mm enhancing extra axial mass just posterior to the V4 segment of the right vertebral artery." That's a medical mouthful. Sounds serious. And yet, the neurodocs blew you off as only incidental.

"Oh, that's no biggie" they would say, "just a little schwannoma."

We never even talk about you in our sessions. The only one to specifically point you out and show us your picture on the monitor was that handsome young Mediterranean intern we saw one time in Bernie's consult room who captivated us by expertly maneuvering and navigating through the hundreds of images of my brain on his large computer monitor.

The little schwannoma, not worthy of a name.

"She is not your problem." I am told by the doctors.

It is your big sis Pinena who is the troublemaker. But I decide to bring your character into the story anyway. You will serve as a constant gratitude reminder, living inside my head. Your name is Pollyanna. You are not of this century, but you are a classic.

I've been called a Pollyanna a time or two, usually in a pejorative way. I was being too naive or unrealistic, always putting a positive spin on everything. The original Pollyanna, a character in Eleanor Porter's classic children's story was treated very differently in her day. She was the first to put her faith in gratitude. She used to play a game called *The Glad Game*. This game was a very simple act of finding something to be grateful about, in everything that happens.

She explained. "The game was just to find something to be glad about, no matter what 'twas." Like growing a brain tumor or two.

CHAPTER 5: THE WORLD BEFORE BS
(BRAIN SURGERY)

My story is now divided into two parts, before and after the BS (brain surgery). Life until the point of BS was very fortunate. It was easy breezy and everything was mostly all right. I moved merrily along, taking my status quo good life for granted. I believed I called my own shots, made my own decisions and was in control of most, if not all, aspects of my lovely life. Soon I will learn that these beliefs about being in control will need to be dropped as I try to solve my brain tumor dilemma. I can take nothing and no one for granted, but I don't know that yet.

I retired early from my job as a human resources trainer and employee relations manager in public education. The job was slowly chipping away at my soul. After that, the part-time reference librarian job I thought would be my dream retirement job didn't quite work out. I discovered I liked hanging out in libraries much more than enforcing library rules. So I took a leap, submitted my resignation and decided to trust the next chapter would reveal itself.

At my retirement party, people asked what I planned to do with my time.

"Sit on my couch and chill."

Books and reading are my biggest pleasures and I spent loads of my time reading tons of books. I took long dog walks. I watched too much MSNBC and the Real Housewives. Yes, I say without irony that I watched and laughed with the Real Housewives. Who can't love a franchise when one of the New Jersey housewives' tag line is "Namaste, bitches?" I went out to lunch with friends, went to the movies, played Scrabble and joined a Buddhist meditation group.

Life inside my bubble was all comfort and stability. Retirement was slow and beautiful. Because I needed to supplement my modest early retirement pension, I also entered the world of part-time odd jobs. One thing I was certain about was not wanting to be in a professional academic environment anymore. I tried my hand at plant merchandising. Arranging, watering, fertilizing and pruning plants was quite enjoyable. But I soon discovered I wasn't physically strong enough to lift the tall glazed ceramic garden pots shipped in every week from Vietnam.

Once I unwrapped the beautiful pottery from their thin delicate brown paper, tied with natural hemp string, my ninety-five-pound, five-foot frame was no match for moving or artfully arranging these hundred-pound vessels among the philodendron and ferns. I quit after three months of physical labor, exhausted.

Next, I managed to find a less physical job that I was not at all qualified for, an online facilitator of mindfulness training for people suffering from depression and anxiety. In preparation, I did what I always do when in over my head, I read. I dove into all kinds of books on mindfulness, meditation and mental health.

Jon Kabat Zinn's books were stacked up on my night stand. He is the granddaddy of popularizing Buddhism with his mindfulness-based stress reduction for mental health. Sylvia Boorstein's *Funny, You Don't Look Buddhist* book sat in my purse and I would read and reread it when stuck in traffic or standing in grocery store lines. One of my favorites was Timber Hawkeye's *Buddhist Boot Camp* because of its plain language writing. His Buddhist teaching is shared in clear and easy-to-understand language. I wondered then and I wonder still why so many

Jews, like me, are attracted to psycho-therapeutic
Buddhism and mindfulness.

Listening to recordings of talks by Alan Watts, Thich
Nhat Hanh and other dharma teachers accompanied every
dog walk and many car rides. All the teachers seemed to be
saying the same thing. Stay in the here and now and
breathe. Their talks reminded me of a piece of wisdom
imparted to me by Grammy, my maternal grandmother
who lived to be one hundred and one years old. When she
was a mere one hundred, one day she declared:

"Susie, I'm going to tell you the secret to living a long
life." she said.

I perked up and leaned in, ready to receive her wisdom.

"You keep breathing."

Grammy had a sense of humor and an abiding wisdom.
Former monk Jay Shetty writes in his book, *Think Like a
Monk*, the first thing monks are taught in school is how to
breathe because, he explains, it is the only thing that stays
with you from the moment you are born until the moment
you die.

Grammy taught me about wabi-sabi too, but with a
Jewish twist. Whenever I would complain about some

triviality in one of our many conversations, she would remind me, "Susan, don't let the perfect be the enemy of the good." She added the instructive "don't let" to this aphorism commonly attributed to Voltaire because Jewish grandmothers tend to be a bit bossy.

In this moment, with just this breath, you have everything you need. It always comes back to the breath. The 4-Square: Let out all the air from your lungs, hold for a count of 4. Take a deep breath in through the nose for 4 seconds. Hold for 4 seconds. Exhale through the mouth as you count to 4, hold for 4. Inhale/exhale. Repeat until you feel a sense of calm. Other than your mind's noise and chattering thoughts, where is the problem? Or, in the classic words of spiritual teacher Ram Dass, "Be here now."

The part-time facilitator job became the proverbial "teach what you need to learn." My clients were from all over the world and were, for the most part, bright and interesting. They had no idea how much they were teaching me. The only part of the job I didn't like was their growing dependency on me. The structure and curriculum were designed to facilitate self-help, but the participants looked to me as their expert and didn't seem to gel as a group if I didn't take an active leadership role. I worried they were becoming overly dependent because I knew I wouldn't be staying long. That was the beauty of part-time retirement odd jobs. Easy come and easy go.

After a few years, I gave up the mindfulness facilitator gig to take on more responsibilities for my mother who was in her end-of-life Parkinson's disease journey. Traveling back and forth to Phoenix where she was living at the time and rushing to get back in time for the evening mindfulness sessions became one stressor I decided to let go of. I was feeling so pressured that I couldn't even appreciate the irony that getting to the mindfulness teaching on time had become a major cause of stress.

Although I had no literary aspirations, reading is and was one of my deepest pleasures. I belonged to, and still do, two book clubs, one secular and one spiritual. The secular club is a wonderful group of avid reading ladies. Every member of our club, aside from me, is an excellent cook. We read and discuss books, but mostly we eat, drink and enjoy each other's company. I briefly attended a spiritual book study of the ancient sacred Jewish text, the Talmud, with the local Chabad Rabbi. Hoping to find the ancient wisdom relevant for my spiritual curiosities, I soon lost interest with the overwhelming Jewish minutiae. I struggled to understand why the smallest of details mattered while at the same time feeling a sense of being part of something bigger that in many ways explains who I am.

From the outside, things looked pretty good. Life was safe. It was predictable, easy and pleasant. But I was not really awake. I didn't yet know it, but deep inside the middle of my brain, things were going wrong and chaos was about to explode. I was taking the comfort of the good life and my privilege for granted, almost like a small child, blissfully unaware of how quickly life could change and relatively good health could disappear. I still have shame about taking so much for granted, but I know now it was paving the way for a more spiritual awareness. It would take a little emergency brain surgery to fully wake me up to profound gratitude.

Weekends were spent with my boyfriend, Cameron. We alternated houses, doing sleepovers with each other and our pets. Owning our own separate homes was our key for going beyond my "ten years and out" history of live-in relationships and his three failed attempts at marriage. Having our own houses meant our time spent together was all light and fun. We had no shared home responsibilities so there were never disagreements about what needed to be done in maintaining, cleaning, organizing or decorating the house.

When I got tired of the clutter in his house or the rusty car parts soaking in the kitchen sink, I could retreat back to my clutter-free cabin in the woods. When he felt confined in my minimalist (yet warm and inviting) cabin, he could retreat back over the mountain to his garage and tools. Our separate houses are on either side of a big mountain called Mingus. People would tell us all the time how envious they were of our arrangement, the best of both worlds. Our relationship was one of mutual independence and we joked that we were the happy bi-Mingual couple. Even though we are now living together on his side of the mountain, a year after brain surgery, I haven't given up my cabin in the woods retreat.

Our separate quarters arrangement worked out beautifully for twelve happy, easy and carefree years. We were in love and life was good. On our thirteenth lucky and unlucky year, everything would change. In place of the carefree life, we would reach new levels of intimacy unknown to us before through a medical trauma and surgical miracle. He would step up and sign on as my full-time live-in caregiver and supervisor. If he hadn't agreed to this new arrangement required by my medical team, I could not be discharged from my brain surgery hospital bed. This part of the story will come later. My boyfriend is my Zen rock. He calms me down, walks me off the ledge and carries me through the storm.

Meanwhile, with all the comfort and ease in the before BS era, I was also suffering with an auto-immune inflammatory arthritis condition. I mostly tried to pretend like it was no big deal. My hyperactive immune system was going haywire and attacking my own body. I was diagnosed with a disease called Ankylosing Spondylitis (autoimmune arthritis) by three different rheumatologists. It is basically a fancy name for arthritis, but it is caused by inflammation rather than aging or mechanical wear and tear. It was explained to me as a progressive disease and I was prescribed immune-suppressing biologic pharmaceuticals to treat it. I refused these drugs.

All three doctors handed me identical glossy color brochures with images of curved spinal columns. I wonder who pays for these expensive publications. Big Pharma? I read the brochures and researched the disease. I learned about the potential side effects of the biologic drugs and decided to hold off taking them for as long as possible. The drugs suppress the immune system and create a higher risk for inviting in all kinds of infections. The known and unknown potential side effects sounded much worse than any of my symptoms.

I designed my own plan for keeping the disease at bay, which included hiking with my dog, moving my body as often as I could, eating more berries, nuts, oily fish, walnuts and anti-inflammatory cruciferous veggies. I cooked with olive oil and added fish oil, turmeric and ginger supplements to my diet. Ironically, I was trying to boost my overactive immune system, even though the doctors were prescribing drugs to suppress it.

I believe strengthening rather than suppressing my immune system is more important than it has ever been now that I am living with brain tumors. I want to discourage, not encourage, more unwanted guests. Even though I can't get any of my brilliant neurodocs to show interest in the connections between my off-the-scale inflammation and my brain tumors, Pinena tells me differently. There is.

My decision to take a conservative approach to my inflammatory disease was not supported by the medical community. One rheumatologist advised starting out slow with a dmard, a drug that suppresses the immune system called Methotrexate. He said it would slow the disease progression but said nothing about alleviating muscle pain or joint stiffness.

"What's a dmard?"

"It's a disease modifying anti rheumatic drug."

"Oh, but I don't really have a full-blown disease."

"Oh, you will."

It is amazing how words said so casually can stay with you for years, words the speaker probably doesn't even remember saying. Another rheumatologist asked me why I was wasting her time if I wasn't interested in the biologic option. She didn't put it quite that rudely, but I got the message.

I was sure my aches, pains and stiffness from my inflammatory disease could be managed with long dog walks in the woods, over-the-counter anti-inflammatory meds, rest, relaxation, reading and mindfulness. My companion dog Paisley would be a big supporter of this plan. She is always up for a walkie or down for a nap. And she is a great teacher and role model for in-the-moment living.

Providing companionship and care for my mother Molly on her end-of-life journey was taking up more and more of my time She was suffering from Parkinson's disease and living in an assisted living facility about an hour and half away from my home. I took her to doctor appointments, visited her often and spoke to her by phone several times a day. We had a complicated relationship. I was resentful but dutiful in serving as her caregiver. We were in a strange type of competition with one another, each outdoing the other in our resentments and lack of gratitude, and very much entwined in each other's lives.

On one of my visits, I found Molly riding up and down her facility corridors on her candy apple red Jazzy-brand motorized scooter. It was full of scrapes and scratches, but she had discovered the magic of black sharpie pens and used it well to meticulously cover up the dents and dings. Ironically, years later, I would end up doing basically the same thing with my car when I mysteriously lost the ability to maneuver in and out of my garage without sideswiping its narrow walls. Me, my mother, her scooter and my car, we were all a little scuffed up.

One day Molly and I were traveling side by side, moving slowly and steadily down a wide hallway in a common area. I was on her left side, walking next to her as she drove her motorized scooter. Suddenly and without warning, she made a hard-left turn and pinned me up against the wall. I grabbed onto the scooter handlebars, trying my hardest to push her away, yelling,

"Back it the fu%k up, Mom!"

She was laughing hysterically, going full throttle forward. She held nothing back, seemingly unaware of the potential pain or injury.

I suppose it was an involuntary Parkinson's spasm that triggered the sudden move, but I couldn't find my compassion in that moment. I do remember it struck me as the life metaphor for our challenging and ungrateful relationship.

For us, everything always hovered on the edge of disaster or defeat, yet we both still knew we would always be there for each other. As I write my story, I feel rushes of gratitude for her and guilt for criticizing her in these pages. Jewish guilt is like bedrock. It runs deep. She was just an anxious and frightened single mom, probably undiagnosed for depression and obsessive-compulsive disorder so sadly untreated. She would reject any kind of psychological clinical language or mention of mental health as weakness to be overcome by sheer will and fervent denial. My life has been safe and privileged, largely because of her.

Later, through my education and healing work on the wounds of brain surgery and tumors, I will find profound gratitude for the privilege and honor of serving as her sole (and soul) companion in the final two years of her life. I owe this gratitude, in part, to doing the internal work of healing the mother wound. I am now too stiff with age and filled with brain tumor insight to do any further bowing down to her. Now, I can just love her. Finally, in hindsight, I can see how overwhelmed, exhausted and unwell she was.

Now I can find nothing left in my heart for her but compassion.

Chapter 6: Wet, Wobbly and Wacky

*When things are desperate, there is
no need to pretend that everything is beautiful.*
– His Holiness, the Dalai Lama

I didn't have a near-death experience, but I descended into something even worse (in my mind). It was the loss of control of mind and body. I could no longer deny noticing things in my body were failing. I had been pretending for a few years, but my symptoms were progressing. I was pretty sure it wasn't "just" the autoimmune disease of inflammatory arthritis. Subconsciously I suspected something more sinister was at play. It was becoming impossible to keep soldiering on.

The over-the-counter anti-inflammatory meds were no longer working. I was slower, stiffer and wobblier. I was sluggish all the time. I felt like I was walking under water, moving in slow motion, sometimes slogging through mud. I would experience bouts of what I called forward momentum. I couldn't slow down or stop moving forward unless I could find a tree, a fence or anything in my path to grab onto to break my movement.

The good life was interrupted by physical pain and limited mobility. Walking my dog Paisley our 10,000 steps a day became painful at first and then impossible. Extreme fatigue kicked in way before the walks ended. I no longer trusted my balance. My brain was foggy. I wasn't thinking straight. I would forget to pick up the mail on the way home from the walk or forget whether or not I fed the dog. I started making checklists but forgot to check things off the list when done. Reading my beloved books was out. I would reread pages, forget plot lines and wasn't retaining anything I read.

On one of my regular daily morning walks I couldn't make it home in time to pee. I wet myself, urine soaking my jeans. It wasn't a small leakage; it was a deluge. I took off my clothes, tossed them in the washer, jumped in the shower and vowed not to drink so much coffee before the next walk. After that, I was embarrassed and made up excuses so I wouldn't have to walk with neighbors or stop to chat. This was definitely something new happening.

My sacroiliac joints were on fire and my lower back felt

stiff all day long. It was no longer loosening up the way it used to after a walk. I couldn't turn my neck without turning my whole body. I felt old. I didn't trust my body, but was becoming more aware of my body sensations. It was taking me longer to get up off the couch. Once I stood up, I had to stand in place and wait for the sacroiliac joints to calm down before I could take a step or walk. Gliding across the hardwood floors in socks felt more comfortable than picking up my feet when walking from room to room. Sliding helped to steady my wobbly gait.

Anyone would have been worried with these increasing symptoms of pain and limited mobility. But I was exceptionally anxious because I had seen all of these symptoms in my mother, five or six years before. I still clearly remember watching the progression of her Parkinson's disease attack her body when I was caring for her in the last few years of her life. The ugliness of Parkinson's disease ravaging my mother started dominating my thoughts. I immediately went to my place of anxiety, silently asking myself, "What will I do if I have Parkinson's?"

Memory lapses were getting harder to deny. I would

have trouble remembering where I parked my car in store parking lots. Things were definitely changing, but I was also still in denial, which is a pretty powerful tool. I would laugh off the car damage after side swiping my garage walls to "old lady driver syndrome." Cameron spent hours and hours fixing and painting it right for me. One day he got pretty angry, which he rarely does, and refused to fix it any more. He said it wasn't worth his time and energy since I kept crashing around and ruining all his beautiful work. I understood. I convinced myself I didn't really mind the bumps and ugly gashes. Later Cameron would feel guilty for getting angry with me when we learned it was Pinena the brain tumor in the driver's seat.

Since I was still not on board with the rheumatologist's solution of biologic drugs, I decided to make an appointment with my primary care doctor. Maybe she could refer me to a physical therapy program to help improve my mobility and gait issues. I told her I was having more difficulty with walking and feeling extremely fatigued.

"We don't have a drug to make you not tired." she said.

I made a mental note to find a new doctor as soon as I could find more energy to do the search.

She handed me a pamphlet on plant-based diets along with a referral slip for physical therapy and wished me well. I felt dismissed and wondered whether I was just being a whiner or a hypochondriac.

I only came in to see this doctor once a year for an annual wellness visit. I phoned in lab test requests for her to order my blood work to measure inflammation markers every three or four months. It wasn't like I was taking up a whole lot of her time. Her dismissal of my fatigue complaints and general lack of interest in the off-the-scale inflammation markers added to my growing distrust of the medical profession in general.

The distrust was around opposite responses from doctors, but it was starting to run deep and wide. This primary care doctor seemed to be blowing off my symptoms. The rheumatology specialists were pushing expensive biological drugs to treat inflammatory arthritis that often leave patients more susceptible to infections and other serious side effects.

I followed up with the physical therapy appointment. The therapist had me walk back and forth as she observed my gait and had me show her my daily stretching routine.

"Are you worried about losing your balance?"

She said I walked with a tentativeness that looked like I was afraid of falling.

She recommended changing one part of a modified sit up in my stretching routine because it may have been aggravating my back. Other than that, she said I seemed pretty strong and healthy.

So why did I feel like crap and why was I exhausted all the time? Disheartened, I decided to go back into my bubble of denial, pop a few more over-the-counter anti-inflammatory pills, make Port-O-Potty stops in the park on my walks and soldier on.

Self-Diagnosing and Misdiagnoses

My decline gradually continued and eventually my mobility deteriorated to the point where I could no longer walk Paisley on my own. I had to ask Cameron for help. I packed a bag and decided to stay at his house for a while. It no longer felt safe staying on my own.

Along with my clothes, I packed paperwork for filing my tax returns and made an appointment to get the returns filed with the AARP folks in Sedona this year, instead of

Prescott. I forgot that appointment and made another at a different AARP site in Camp Verde. I missed that appointment too and finally missed the April 15 filing date. I couldn't think straight. I couldn't walk. I wasn't even sure what year it was. I have never missed filing income taxes in my forty plus years of filing. I didn't care. I ended up eventually paying a late penalty. Apparently, not knowing what year we are in doesn't cut it as an excuse for not filing taxes.

At this point, I convinced myself I had Parkinson's disease. My symptoms were presenting just like my Mom's. As my health was declining, I was consulting over the phone with my bestie Jersey Girl, Elisa. She is a crackerjack physical therapist but I treat her like my personal doctor. We talked about treatments and programs I might look into for managing my self-diagnosed Parkinson's and came up with two programs popular for treating the disease. Boxing was one, but neither of us could envision me bobbing and weaving or pounding a punching bag. I understood the value of the speed and the foot-work, but with my poor balance it was just too scary. And it wasn't me.

The other program she recommended was called *Big and Loud.* It is a physical therapy program that helps patients with Parkinson's disease improve slow motor and cognitive functions through exercise and patient empowerment. Sounded perfect. I found a class being offered in nearby Sedona and called to sign myself up. The receptionist took my information over the phone and said I would be covered by insurance. To get started, all they needed was the doctor's diagnosis and referral.

"Oh, I am self-diagnosed." I said.

I thought I could hear a bit of stifled laughter on the other end of the phone.

"Yeah, that's not gonna work for us."

I told the receptionist I would be willing to do the class as a self-pay. That wouldn't be possible either because of liability issues. No fucking wonder I was having a hard time trusting this medical profession. Looking back, thank G-d I didn't get into the class because *Big and Loud* classes incorporated some boxing moves to work on movement and speed. That meant I could have been boxing Pinena.

I was slowly losing control of my mind and body and getting nowhere with my local medical community. I decided to make an appointment with a movement specialist at the Mayo Clinic in Phoenix. They are known to be the best in the world for diagnostics. The appointment would be eight weeks out.

Rather than sit and wait for the Mayo Clinic appointment, Cameron suggested we take a road trip to Lake Havasu, Arizona. I agreed it might be a nice distraction from feeling so sick and tired. He had seen a used big rig RV for sale online. We already had a small Class C-motor home, but he thought a larger one might be better for longer trips. On our last road trip, I kept mysteriously banging my head on the overhead sleeping bunk. A brain tumor diagnosis would solve the head banging mystery, but it wouldn't come for several more months.

Lake Havasu is a hot spot and even though it was only April, it was already over 100 degrees. Arizona, it's a dry heat. Right. It's the kind of heat where it is not a myth or a cliché to fry an egg on the sidewalk. There is actually an annual 4th of July sidewalk egg fry competition in the small town of Oatman, Arizona, less than fifty miles north of Lake Havasu.

While Cameron checked out the used big rig and

negotiated the price with the sales guy, I decided to take Paisley on a walk. We wandered outside of the Sunshine RV Store and aimlessly roamed around the industrial neighborhood. Under my breath, I chanted "Sunshine RV, Sunshine RV, Sunshine RV", over and over so I wouldn't forget where we were. The intense heat beat down on us and I tried to create a mnemonic in my mind, linking the blazing sun with the name Sunshine RV to remember the name of the store. My brain wasn't functioning well, but I wasn't yet aware of the degree of the cognitive decline.

I was grateful to find my way back to the RV Store and find Cameron. He was excited about the deal he just made. The sales guy took a look at me, showed me a chair and handed me a bottled water. I guzzled it down in practically one large gulp. I then turned to Cameron and asked,

"Did you bring me here to die?"

I still don't know what I meant when I asked this question. Maybe it was the beginning of intuitively understanding how sick I was.

When we got back home, I kept losing my balance and tripping over throw rugs, doorway thresholds, steps and dog beds. I understood my independence was disappearing and

I was becoming fearful of losing total control of my body and my mind. At the same time, I was grateful for Cameron. He was watching my every move, making sure to catch me when I stumbled backwards. I was understanding that I could not possibly live independently anymore. I worried that I had become a burden. I worried he would leave me. Our perfect stress-free arrangement of separate houses and fun on weekends had disappeared. Just like that.

Cameron never once complained. I am sure he had a lot of thoughts and feelings about my condition. Later he told me he was worried about the future and if I would ever get better. And he felt sad about my limitations and pain.

He would rather I didn't write about him. He doesn't like the attention or the praise. But this is his story too. Maybe it's what the New Zealanders call the *Tall Poppy Syndrome*. His family roots are from New Zealand. *Tall Poppies* is a cultural phenomenon that promotes modesty and mocks people who think too highly of themselves.

He never made the "in sickness or in health" vow to me in front of G-d (he's an atheist), a rabbi, family or friends. He shows me his unwavering commitment, every single day. When I see him, I am instantly calmed. Becoming so vulnerable with Cameron, through no choice of my own, had the unintended consequence of us reaching new levels of intimacy together. At first, I found his devotion over-whelming. I didn't see the emotional growth it would create or the way it would grow our relationship. We are both pretty commitment phobic. His unavailability was something I found attractive when we first met. When he told me he was separated, not yet divorced, my first thought was "perfect, I love unavailable men."

We're still working on our ability to verbalize commit-ment. Ours is more of a show don't tell kind of thing.

Recently I said, "Isn't it strange how we just sort of moved in and are living together now?"

"Are we? I thought you were just staying for a while."

We laugh. I still worry that I am a post-op brain tumor patient burden on him. I think the real burden is that I continue to ask if I am a burden. I want to be more of a partner and a better one. The instant I switch from a show don't tell devotion to my neurotic need for love and approval, it stops our newfound intimacy in its tracks. I don't want to go back there, no matter where I ultimately end up living. I don't have words to express the enormity of my gratitude and love for this very special man.

One evening, after another fall in the bathroom, I called my brother. He spoke with Cameron and the decision was made to take me to the Verde Valley Medical Center's Emergency Room. I was given a CT scan, a diagnosis of hydrocephalus, issued a walker and told to follow up with my primary care doctor to schedule an MRI.

I googled "hydrocephalus":

1. Incontinence. Check.
2. Balance problems and gait disturbance. Check.
3. Cognitive impairment. Check.

I prefer the demonic mnemonic of wet, wobbly and wacky:

Wet is when finding restrooms wherever you go becomes second nature. I can tell you where the public restrooms are located in every shop, restaurant, and place I patronize. This kind of wet isn't the kind of leakage you hear women of a certain age talk about happening when they laugh too hard or sneeze. This is a steady stream, a soaking, not a trickle or leak.

I tried doing Kegel exercises five or six times a day to

try to strengthen my bladder. It didn't matter how many I could do; it would not have made a difference. It wasn't the bladder; it was the brain.

Years earlier I tried explaining to my mother that her incontinence wasn't a faulty bladder, but rather a Parkinson's brain problem. She didn't want to listen back then because she was excited about finding a urologist who was willing to do exploratory bladder surgery on her.

When you are the wet, wobbly and wacky one, it is easier to understand and feel compassion.

This is the kind of wet that keeps the "discreet underwear" *Always* as a recurring item on the shopping list and a hefty supply of packages under the bathroom sink. Once when Cameron was unpacking our groceries, he handed me the pack of *Always*. I handed him back my Kindle with a YouTube video playing Stevie Wonder singing *I'll Be Loving You Always* from *Songs in the Key of Life* and asked him, "Should this be our song?"

Humor and the blessing of laughter goes a long way in the most painful and humiliating situations. I continue to take this wisdom to heart.

Wobbly: is when you trip going up the stairs, rather

than down. It is when you secretly lust after the steady bars you watch your boyfriend install in his ninety-eight-year-old Dad's shower stall. It's when you are brought to tears watching your best friend assemble the candy apple red Rollater walker he found on sale at Walgreens and brought home to you as a surprise. Or when the same best friend sends you home with a big ugly white plastic shower chair instead of the usual home-made desserts, he made the night before.

Wacky: is buying three pretty pocket calendars but missing your hair, eye exam and dentist appointments. It's paying your utility and cable bills twice. And it's the look you get from loved ones when you repeat stories they are too embarrassed to tell you they've heard before. I know what happens when memory ends, balance fails and your bladder stops working.

I had been thrust into a land of primal fear; dementia, incontinence and a shuffling gait.

I was used to living independently, but Cameron had taken over most aspects of my life because I trusted him more than myself. All I could do was lay on the couch and worry about how my life was over. I lost all independence. I couldn't think straight. I could barely walk. Trusting my life to another was something new and scary, but oddly spiritual too.

Cameron set up my household bills on autopay because we discovered I was paying utility bills twice. He tried his best, but ultimately even he failed to arrange for my MRI to be done locally. Too much red tape within the local medical community and insurance world.

Navigating the medical maze of insurance, referrals, appointments and trying to get any kind of follow-through with my primary care doctor proved to be an impossible task. We couldn't get the primary care physician to connect with the insurance folks. She scolded Cameron for calling her on her cell phone, a number we pulled from a call she made to me on my cell phone. I didn't realize that I was calling her over and over and then forgetting we had spoken. He wanted to tell her, "She doesn't remember calling you. Can't you see this is cognitive decline?" Instead, he wrote her off as useless, moved on and still doesn't have the time of day for her. I lost all trust in the medical profession, or at least my so-called primary care.

Cameron doesn't easily give up. After giving the earful

to my primary doctor, he coached me on calling the Mayo Clinic back to try and get an earlier appointment, thinking we might have more luck with the specialists there. He wanted to make this happen, but he also wanted to do his best at supporting whatever little bit of independence I could maintain. He thought it best if I could make the call myself and try to get the appointment moved up.

He helped me dial the Mayo Clinic number and listened in as I spoke, ready to take the phone back if it looked like I wasn't capable of explaining the situation or remembering what was said to me. Fortunately, I was able to move the appointment up. But I could only be scheduled to see a resident neurologist, rather than a movement disorder specialist. Fine by me, just get me in to see someone, and the sooner the better, because I could not live this way a day longer.

CHAPTER 7: ARRIVING AT THE EMERALD CITY (AKA THE MARVELOUS MAYO CLINIC)

You Have A Brain Tumor. Wait, What?!

In the brain tumor community, the Mayo Clinic (https://www.mayoclinic.org/) is known as the Emerald City. It is a magical place and, like its iconic namesake, has a brightness and glory. Most times, a pianist plays live classical music on a grand piano as you enter into the lobby. The staff are professional and friendly, the systems and processes are efficient, unlike any of the local doctor's offices I've ever visited. I arrive at the Emerald City with the innocence of Dorothy, not yet aware of how my journey will ultimately morph into becoming Alice, where I'll find myself going through the looking glass, in a curiouser and curiouser world. And my ruby red slippers will be regulation issued non-skid slippers, color-coded ruby red to indicate "fall risk."

If you're sick and need treatment, this is the only place to be. They are the diagnostic specialists and I only wish I could have them as my primary care doctors instead of just my specialists. They are true to the values stated in their humanitarian mission of healing, inspiring hope and nurturing the well-being of the whole person, respecting physical, emotional and spiritual needs of patients.

We arrived at the off-site parking in our new Dolphin brand RV, which we rebranded Dolphin-Care because it was converted into my new health facility. We were staying in the RV Park of the West World event facility in the desert in Scottsdale, Arizona, at the base of the McDowell mountains. Cameron picked this spot because it was out of the way, spacious and just a few miles from the Mayo Clinic.

Our pets Paisley and Rom were enjoying the new digs and the adventure. I may have been enjoying the new larger RV space too, but most of my memories are clouded. It felt very roomy and much more comfortable than our old smaller Class-C motor home, but I could not seem to get comfortable. My head felt so heavy, it was hard to sit up without falling over to one side. I understand now why I had started to regularly bump my head on the frame of the sleeping area above the cab in the old motor home. My head was literally drowning in fluid buildup.

A low point of this trip would happen right away in the hard, cold tiled floors in the public shower building. Even though our space had full hookups with unlimited water, I decided to use the public showers to wash my hair because I wanted unlimited hot water too. I wasn't used to having bigger tanks yet and remembered running out of hot water in the old RV before my hair was fully rinsed. I have a lot of hair. Cameron stood guard in front of the women's public showers, holding Paisley, and I entered the building with my shampoo and my walker.

I don't remember what happened next. Memory loss can be a merciful thing. As Cameron tells it, a woman came out of the building and said to him,

"She needs help in there."

He had been standing just outside the shower doors, listening for me and calling out every few minutes to make sure I was OK, until she came along. When he saw her approach the building, he moved slightly away from the entrance. He didn't want to appear to be a creepy man alone, lurking in front of a women's shower room, even if he was holding onto the cutest spotted rescue dog alive.

When he entered the building, he found me on the floor, naked butt pointing straight up in the air, towel wrapped around my head, turban-style. I couldn't tell him what happened, I had no idea how I ended up on the floor. He checked me out for injuries and then got me up and dressed. We headed back to the RV, me on my walker and Cameron walking Paisley beside me. He was lecturing about public showers.

"See why I don't want you using the public showers?"

He put his foot down, which isn't at all like him, and declared,

"That's it. All future showers will be done in the safety of the RV."

I sure wasn't in a position to argue that one.

Later, we would reflect on my good luck for not falling on my head and cracking open my skull. Of course, this was before we knew my skull would soon be cracked open, but not on a hard tile shower floor.

Seeds of Trust in The Medical World Sprout in The Emerald City

My first appointment at the Marvelous Mayo was with a young neurologist resident whose name I can't remember. He gave me the first of what turned out to be many neurological assessments. Touch my finger. Touch your nose. Pull my hand. Push me away. Follow my finger up. Down. Left and now right. Stand still and close your eyes.

He gave me a little push forward and then lightly pulled me back to see how my balance was holding. To all of our surprise, the backwards pull startled me so much that I toppled backwards, almost hitting the floor. The resident doctor caught me in his arms before I hit the floor. This was followed by me having an emotional breakdown and a good old ugly cry, right there on the consult room floor.

The resident's supervisor later apologized for the experience. The resident told him I had a rather rough time in the exam. I remember feeling sorry for the resident because I am sure it was also rough on him. I was sent for an MRI, another CT scan and a spinal tap. I don't remember the order.

Bernie, April-May, 2019

After my tests, through the grace of G-d, and an unbelievable amount of luck, my fate was decided with a referral to neurosurgery. Enter the elite and talented Chief of Neurosurgery who resides in the basement offices in Building1, inside the cool air-conditioning of the Emerald City. Dr. Bernard Bendok. The Boss. Bernie. The Kintsugi artist who saved my life.

I don't remember getting checked in or being escorted into a consult room. I only remember my world being rocked when a tall man with an olive complexion, a shaved head and compassionate eyes, wearing a crisp white doctor coat, outstretched a hand and introduced himself. Then he said five words that changed my life forever.

"You. Have. A. Brain. Tumor."

Wait, what?!? Cameron and I looked at each other. All expression drained from our faces. We had the same thought: "This shit just got real."

Before having any time to digest the shock we had just been handed, Bernie went on to explain the ETV procedure he would perform on my broken brain.

"First things first, we will fix the hydrocephalus."

Looking back, I marvel over how he was able to figure these impossible things out. He said he would try to get a tumor biopsy while he was inside my brain, but couldn't make any promises. The pineal gland brain tumor was lodged deep in the center of the brain, surrounded by a bunch of neurovascular structures. Apparently, the odds of the angle and danger of reaching it were pretty slim and steep. It made for a difficult path to reach and he said he would have a low threshold for going in so deep if it didn't look straightforward.

He said we needed a biopsy in order to have definitive knowledge of the tumor's pathology. If he wasn't able to do that, then he would bring me back in at a later time for a second round. I never heard him say second round. Later, I would be aggrieved when he would bring it up as a possibility at our first post-surgical meeting. I only learned about this initial plan when I read the report in my portal, while doing research for this memoir, a full year later.

Not only did I not hear it, but somehow, somewhere along my journey I adopted a core belief. I made a vow. My vow came right off of my favorite black hoodie sweatshirt purchased online from the Hydrocephalus Association (https://www.hydroassoc.org/). It's kind of a funny slogan and I made it my own. The blue wave graphic reads: "No More BS (brain surgery)."

I hoped Cameron was listening to Bernie because I was only hearing about every third or fourth word. My mind wandered in and out of the conversation. He may have told me about a smaller tumor on my brain stem called a schwannoma. He may have said it wasn't worrisome. I guess I decided to forget about that one for now.

The big and troublesome tumor was a two-centimeter mass deep inside my pineal gland. That is the only one I remembered. It was causing all of my symptoms by obstructing the flow of brain fluid. He explained the risks involved in surgery, bleeding being the worst. Fortunately, my cognitive state was at an all-time low, so I really wasn't taking in too much of what he was saying. I had the mercy of memory loss. Cameron did not.

We don't know this yet, but Bernie will save my life. He will open up my head, touch places that control memories, movement, body functions and personality. He will work his magic and I will walk again, think clearly, have a fully functioning bladder and be a more grateful person. It is easy to want to imbue him as a wise, all-knowing being with great mystical powers. I pretty much worship him. Is this idolatry, I wonder? Oh well, I am pretty sure G-d forgives me.

My, Oh My, A Reservoir; My Ommaya Reservoir

Ommaya reservoir: a device implanted in the brain for instillation of medication or removal of fluid through a catheter in a lateral ventricle, attached to a reservoir implanted under the scalp.

The man who was proposing to penetrate my skull and probe around my brain went on to explain how he would be implanting an Ommaya reservoir before leaving my head. I had stopped listening. It would be months before I had a clue what an Ommaya reservoir was or why he thought I needed one. I just made up a happy-ever-after story that made it sound like it was a "permanent" fix for the obstructive hydrocephalus. It is not. Nothing is permanent. I didn't have a well-developed wabi-sabi mindset or framework to understand this yet.

The Ommaya reservoir is like an insurance policy. I haven't had to test it out yet, but I am very much aware of its presence.

On the outside it feels like a little dome that pops out of my scalp on the top of my head. Sometimes it tingles. Sometimes it itches. I try to get Cameron to give it a rub, like a genie in a bottle, but he won't. It creeps him out, even though I've told him it might bring him good luck.

When I am in a more metaphorical mood, I refer to it as Bernie's calling card, the ticket stub he left behind after our date in the theater.

When I would first try to explain it to others, I thought it was a device that created a bypass for allowing cerebral spinal fluid to flow freely around the obstructing brain tumor. I loved this little made up story. A creative non-fiction, just like my hopes for this memoir. Then, one day, after an umpteenth time of me explaining how it is like a bypass road around Pinena the tumor, Cameron corrects me. He does this in his inimitable, low key, Zen-like and non-judgmental way.

"I'm not sure you have that right about the Ommaya."

"What do you mean?" I shrieked. "It's called a reservoir. Isn't that what a reservoir does?"

"Yes," he responds calmly. "But I think the hole they poked in your third ventricle is what allows the cerebral spinal fluid flow.

"So what does the Ommaya reservoir do?" I asked.

He shrugged. We are both a bit unsure.

"Well, I like my happy-ever-after story better."

When I am in a more practical mood, it reminds me of the sump pump my Mom had installed under her Phoenix townhouse. She loved that thing and would talk about it with great excitement. When it kicked on during Arizona monsoon seasons, she would call me up and rattle on enthusiastically. It drained the excess water under her house and made her feel safe. It steadied her in the monsoon, which can be a bit scary. Now I find myself rattling on excitedly about my Ommaya reservoir metaphors. It makes me feel safer in a different kind of storm.

It really isn't all that sophisticated of a brain surgery thing. It's more a simple mechanical device. This was finally explained to us one day, on a dog walk, of all places. We stopped to chat with a couple we met on the trail.

We introduced ourselves, had a quick chat about who we are and what we do. The man is a neurologist and his wife had a very positive, upbeat and hilarious energy. We somehow got onto the topic of Ommaya reservoirs. Go figure. I thought it was a state-of-the-art medical device that could only be dealt with at the Marvelous Mayo because of its sophistication. I worried about what might happen if I ever ended up in our small local regional hospital emergency room, needing to be pumped out.

The neurologist educated us on how it was actually quite old technology. It was popular in the eighties, during the AIDS epidemic. He worked in Detroit back in the day and had lots of experience with them. I felt relieved when I learned pumping a reservoir was an older technology, routine and really no big deal. He turned to Cameron, another man, and explained how it was just like a starter button on a lawn mower, making an in and out pumping gesture with his thumb to illustrate. I wonder if that made Cameron feel relief. I don't understand or care about how lawn mowers work. I've never even used one.

As he talked, I was thinking about stuff that interested me, like how much I loved my neurodocs. I blurted out, "Your patients must really love you."

His hilarious wife said,

"Yeah, he comes home and tells me about all his white-haired little old lady patients who all have the same exact hair style." She went on, "Sometimes we sit behind them at musical shows at the local historic opera house. When they are seated next to one another, all in row, their heads look just like a box of Q-tips." She wasn't done yet. She put her hand up just below her husband's chest and said,

"They come up to just about here and always want to embrace him in big hugs."

She went on to say how they smelled like a mix of Jean Naté perfume with a hint of urine. I burst out laughing because I am instantly flooded with incongruous memories of my childhood. I am back in my grandmother's vintage bathroom in her Philadelphia row house. Her Jean Naté perfume products; round silver cardboard talcum powder boxes topped with big powder puffs and bottles of colognes are lined up in neat little rows on the wine-colored tiled shelves on the wall above the toilet.

The neurologist gave me his cell phone number as we were leaving. The kindness of strangers I've met along this journey cracks my heart wide open.

My mind drifts back to the consult room. I hear Bernie telling us before surgery got scheduled, we would be set up for other appointments with a few of his friends so we could benefit from a multi-discipline team approach on our new adventure. He didn't call it an adventure. That's my description. He shook our hands. This was a pre-Covid-19 pandemic time when we could shake hands and hug people. I didn't want to hug him yet, but I already felt his compassion. It wasn't so much in the way he spoke, but you could see it in his eyes. He knew this was a lot for us to take in so he left us alone in the room to process the overwhelming information.

My intuition must not have been completely compromised by the hydrocephalus because I immediately trusted Bernie. Implicitly. I wonder if Pinena had any idea what was coming. I can only imagine what must have been going through Cameron's mind. He didn't have the mercy of being cognitively compromised like me. The people who love and care about patients with serious illness have a lot of the same variety of thoughts and feelings about our condition as we do.

Brain surgery is the hardest kind of surgery because it involves the essence of a person's being. Our souls. It involves touching the places where a person's thoughts, personalities and memories live, not to mention their ability to walk, talk, see, hear and function in every way. Cameron later told me he worried if I would come out of it as the same person.

Meeting Dr. Porter, the first friend of Dr. Kintsugi

April 2019

Dr. Porter was one of Bernie's friends I paid a visit to before my surgery. She was all business. I wondered why or how I got referred to her, other than knowing she was a friend of Bernie's. I looked her up on the Mayo website and discovered she is a neuro-oncologist. Do I have cancer? Isn't it too soon to know that? Cancer was never mentioned before, but maybe I should have just assumed it as a possibility. Shit. What next?

I am confused. My mind flashes back to a conversation I had with a rheumatologist who told me chronic elevated inflammation blood markers like mine are typically seen in the presence of infections, autoimmunity (Ankylosing Spondylitis), trauma and malignancy. Hmm. I still wonder about the possible connections between autoimmune disease and my brain tumor. But that is just an added layer of worry that I needlessly create for myself. I worry when I have nothing to worry about.

Dr. Porter motioned for me to take a seat across the desk, facing her. She came across as serious and no nonsense. There wouldn't be any small talk. I was hardly mobile and used my walker to get to the chair. My brain was foggy and I was confused. She said she would be conducting a neuro-psych evaluation and testing my mental status. I got nervous.

Her first question was checking my general orientation. I was able to tell her we were at the Mayo Clinic in Phoenix and it was the month of April, but I could not tell her the year.

"May I take a quick peek at my pocket calendar?"

"No."

Next, she asked me to draw a clock face showing the time of 11:15. I could do that. Then I was asked to copy an image of a familiar 3-dimensional cube that I used to draw with ease when I was an eight-year-old kid. I could not draw that damn cube.

"Who is our President?"

I let out a deep groan of disgust.

"We get a lot of that lately."

I think I detected a hint of a smile, but she was maintaining a very serious demeanor. Next, she pitched a bunch of math problems out to me.

"What is five multiplied by thirteen?"

I am silent.

"Sixty-five minus seven?"

I am silent.

"Fifty-eight divided by two?"

"May I use a piece of paper and a pen?"

"No," was her answer and said matter-of-factly.

I have difficulty will all the math questions. But I was always crap at math. I probably would have had trouble with those questions when my brain was in top form, which it certainly wasn't today.

"I am going to say four words. Try to remember these words and I will ask you to recite them later. Apple, Mr. Johnson, charity, tunnel."

I can remember only three of them when asked to recall them ten minutes later.

Next, she asks me to try to immediately recall a set of numbers: "Two, nine, six and eighty-three."

I can't. Once again, I sit in silence.

She calls out another set: "Five, seven, one, nine and forty-six."

I look over at Cameron, pleading silently for help. I am sure he is easily remembering these number spans. I can't remember any of them. I want to cry. Dr. Porter closes her notebook. The assessment must be over.

"Once a tissue diagnosis of the pineal mass is done, we will meet again and have a discussion about treatment plans."

I don't remember or think to ask her if I might have cancer. I am too tired. She wishes me well for my upcoming surgery and says she hopes I will enjoy improvements in my gait, balance, bladder and cognitive function once the hydrocephalus is reduced. She uses the formal diagnosis language and I want to joke with her and ask, you mean, wet, wobbly and wacky? I want to lighten things up. We leave her office and I am in a sad, depressed mood with a very foggy brain. I can't think.

"I don't like Dr. Porter very much," I tell Cameron.

I haven't a clue that my opinion of her will make a 180-degree turnaround after surgery. The uneasiness will turn to love and she will become my hero, a beloved advocate and friend in my post-surgical world.

I met a few other friends of Bernie's, a tall Indian man with a kind face who explained radiation and gave me a scary looking booklet with computer generated images of masked heads lying on tables with all kinds of lines and arrows shooting through the body. I don't really remember these meetings, but later I found a small collection of business cards from neuro doctors and nurses stuffed into the side pocket of my purse, the way you would collect business cards from people at a cocktail party who you had no intention of ever calling. I know I also had pre-op bloodwork and an EKG test done to make sure my heart was strong enough for surgery, but I don't remember any of this.

CHAPTER 8: INPATIENT AT
THE MARVELOUS MAYO

D-Day! Surgery! Morning of May 3, 2019

Cognitive decline for me was a blessing and a curse, but ONLY because I was lucky to only get a taste of it. It's only a blessing if it's reversible, which it generally is not. I never want to taste it again. I remember next to nothing about arriving for surgery or getting prepped for the big event. I am mostly filling in with Cameron's memories.

The only thing I do remember is Bernie sitting on my bed and hearing my brother Michael ask him why it would take so long to get pathology lab reports back from the sample of cerebral spinal fluid he planned to extract during the procedure. I didn't understand what they were talking about.

I vaguely remember a German-accented anesthesiologist making breezy jokes. Later Michael would make a joke about him that was in very poor taste. I will leave that one to your imagination. My brother and I share a rather dark and sometimes inappropriate sense of humor, as well 50% common DNA. We get each other.

The surgery was supposed to take up to eight hours. Cameron went out to lunch for vegetarian burgers at a nearby Caribbean restaurant with his daughter and daughter-in-law, Carly and Lilly. They flew in from San Francisco and were staying for a few days. When I first learned they were coming out, I was conflicted. I was happy they wanted to come and support us and I knew it would be wonderful company for Cameron while he waited for all the unknowns.

I really didn't want to see anyone or, rather, have anyone see me, in this condition. They turned out to be the most phenomenal and loving supporters and I don't know what I would have done without them. They are amazing women, kind and generous. They deserve honorary nursing degrees based on their outstanding performance in this adventure.

Cameron hoped the lunch out would be a bit of a distraction from his nerves. Even this eternal optimist was worried. This wasn't only my trauma. They returned from their lunch and settled into a recovery waiting room, surprised to see my name already posted on the electronic patient status board. It had only been two and a half hours.

They met with Bernie in a side room and he told them the 3rd ventriculostomy surgery was successful, but they were not able to biopsy the tumor. The angle was too steep. Cameron says he remembers thanking Bernie, telling him he was an amazing man and wanting to kiss his feet. I know exactly what he means. Only two visitors were allowed back in the recovery area to see me, so Cameron and Carly came in. I didn't remember any of it. I needed to nap.

Evening of May 3, 2019

I am in a lovely single room and allowed my beautiful family and friend visitors. When my brother Michael and sister-in-law Jan came in for a brief visit, I tear up just seeing them. My bestie Greg pops in carrying a small and fabulous pink and white stuffed animal sloth, wrapped up in a tan speckled burrito blanket. I call him Slothritto and curl up to take many recovery naps with him. I am moving at a pace slower than a sloth, but excel at napping. My guests don't stay long since I am tired. I feel overwhelmed with gratitude for being alive and loved.

The first night on the neurological wing is a blur. Nurses come and go every hour and blaring alarms sound off when I attempt to leave the bed. Vital signs are taken every hour, meds administered into painful cannulas attached to both wrists, taped down tight and already showing signs of black and blue bruising. The early morning nurse wakes me up and apologizes before asking me to lift my gown so she can inject a shot of heparin. My tummy is polka dotted with little bruises left behind from all the injections that are meant to prevent clotting.

I am also given an anti-seizure drug called Keppra. Later, I would learn from my fellow brainpeeps this drug can cause terrible side effects like rage, hallucinations and personality changes. Fortunately, I experienced none of these things and was only on the drug for fourteen days. Some folks in the fellowship must stay on it for extended time and it can cause havoc in their lives. Again, I wonder how I can be so lucky.

I have a catheter so there should be no reason to leave the bed. Hellish alarms keep going off and nurses come running whenever I try. They are busy and I don't want to bother them. They tell me it bothers them when I don't ring the call bell. Large posters displayed in the hallways proudly boast a big fat zero under number of falls for the month of May. Their record so far is perfect and this was a success metric they intended to maintain.

I can order off of the room service menu whatever I want for breakfast the next day. I choose oatmeal, coffee, individually cellophane-wrapped graham crackers and a prune juice. When it arrives the next day, I barely touch it because the nausea is back. I prefer a diet of saltines and water. I start to feel better once an anti-nausea patch of Scopolamine is pasted onto the skin just behind my ear. The nurses make sure I always have a handful of the funnel shaped blue plastic barf bags and I used them regularly. It feels secure to know there is a wall dispenser filled with a good supply of them, just off to the side of my bed.

Day Two, May 4, 2019

The day after surgery is a bit of a blur. I have quite a few visitors. My brother and sister-in-law return, as does my beautiful niece Jenn. Carly and Lilly and my bestie Greg come back. Cameron stays most of the day. As soon as I see him walking down the hallway towards my room, I get a surge of gratitude. Happiness and relief wash over my tired body and I feel relaxed in my own skin, ugly hospital gown, wounded head and all. I'd like to bottle this feeling up for when he is gone. Once I texted him at an unG-dly hour of the night to ask him to take me to the loo. He texted back, "I'm not there, ring your bell." I wait for the morning instead.

I loved getting the full report of Paisley and Rom enjoying RV life back at West World. I am so grateful for my family and friends. It is a new feeling of gratitude that I hadn't known or understood at this deep level before this moment. I am touched and I am different, no longer taking any of it for granted.

My room is becoming a bit crowded and loud. I am blabbing away to my visitors about all kinds of medical procedures, symptoms and details while my niece Jenn hangs quietly in the background. When her parents return after taking a quick Starbuck's break, she welcomes them in and advises them.

"Welcome, and just so you know, this hospital room in under the JIPAA, not HIPAA health privacy policy."

"JIPAA?"

"Jewish HIPAA. You tell everybody every detail about your health, and you do it all the time." She is the funniest girl and my go-to person whenever I need a cheering up. Once when Jenn was teaching and I was having a particularly rough recovery day, I phoned her in the middle of her teaching day.

"Tell me something funny. I need to laugh."

"Um, I am teaching now. And it is not something I can just do on demand."

She is more of a situational and observational kind of funny. When I tell her the details about my most amazing first post-surgery shower, she listens intently. I describe how ecstatic it feels to get cleaned up from the sweat, the smell and the caked, dried blood.

My arms are black and blue from the tightly wrapped and ever-present IV cannulas which are still taped to my wrists. I am not supposed to get the IV tubes wet, so I need help in the shower. I explain to Jenn how Cameron and Steve, my calm and adorable neuro-nurse helped me into the shower stall and onto the plastic chair. The warm soapy water was pure heaven. I didn't ever want to get out, but I could see we were creating a small flood because of the poor floor drainage design.

I said, "Cameron and Steve were not enjoying the experience nearly as much as I was."

Jenn said, "So is this how you pictured your first threesome in your fantasy? Inside a shower stall on the neuro ward of the Mayo Hospital?" My head is covered in thick surgical glue, but my niece has me in stitches!

I can't say enough about the kindness, competence, compassion and amazing care I was given by the entire neuro-nursing crew. Down to a person, they were just fantastic and you could tell they really loved their jobs. I had shifted my belief about the medical community. I understood and was now trusting them with my very life. It is very challenging work.

Day Three, May 5, 2019

It's day three, and I finally manage to fall asleep in this disruptive and unnatural setting. The early morning shift nurse apologizes for waking me up, and I sleepily lift my gown, thinking she is here to give me another shot of heparin in my belly. She shakes her head no.

"Sorry to wake you, but the doctors are coming, the doctors are coming."

She says this with urgency, like a Paul Revere "The British are Coming" pronouncement.

"I wanted you to be awake so you don't miss them."

I feel as though she also wants to say, "Maybe you could comb your hair and put on some lipstick?"

That was so sweet of her, but vanity was the last thing on my mind. Doctors rounds are very fast and if you miss them, that's pretty much your problem. You never get advanced notice of when they're going to happen.

Occupational Therapy Evaluation, The Unforgettable Hurricane Hattie

I am told I will be getting a visit from Occupational Therapy (OT) today. I need their evaluation before I can be discharged. When the nurses stop by during the day to check on my vitals they also check to see if I've had my OT visit.

"No, not yet," I say with disappointment.

I know I need an OT evaluation before I can be discharged and I am getting anxious to leave. I wait patiently all day, but no one from OT shows up. I wonder if maybe they forgot about me. I think to myself, *what would my mother Molly do?*

Whatever that is, I should probably do the opposite. This means summoning the will to ignore my natural impulse to call the OT department, complain and demand a visit. I am my mother's daughter, after all.

Meanwhile, there is plenty of distracting activity happening in my room. I have loads of company and visitors. Carly and Lilly are here. Bestie Greg is popping in and out. Jan and Mike stop by to chat and so does Jenn. I love my family and friends. I am grateful for their love and support that I now appreciate on a deeper level. My room is filled with love, laughter and noisy chatter. My brain is having a bit of a hard time processing all the conversations and contending with the noise and hospital hustle bustle. It's too much brain stimulation, but I am grateful to be surrounded by so much love.

And yet, I am still not satisfied. I want my OT visit. Whaa, whaa, whaa.

The next day, a short, attractive, loud Asian woman comes bounding into my room like a micro-burst of energy. Hurricane Hattie. She is shouting at me.

"Why did you say I didn't visit you yesterday? I tried talking to you all afternoon. It's not my fault you wouldn't answer me. You just stared at me with a blank look on your face. I don't know where you were, but you were not there. Put on your slippers, we are going for a walk."

I understood this was not a request, but rather an order. I put my red Mayo non-skid pillow socks on. Hospital socks are color coded. Red means "fall risk." Later, in the less dramatic post-surgical WaWa adventure scenes, I will be issued boring gray colored socks for the regularly scheduled MRIs.

I apologize to Hurricane Hattie for not remembering meeting her yesterday. Her face is starting to look a little familiar. We begin walking around the pod. I am moving slowly on my walker. She takes my elbow, moving me along and quickening our pace.

"Did nobody give you a comb?" What's with that hair? It's a mess! I will fix that."

When we complete one full lap around the pod, she sits me down in a chair in a room off the main hallway.

"Don't move. I will be right back."

And the spitfire ball of energy disappears. Even though I know this chair is not alarmed like the ones in my room, I don't dare move. No telling what Hurricane Hattie might do. Soon she reappears, carrying a plastic cape and a strange portable hair washing system that can be set up right there in the chair, without a sink.

"I am going to wash your hair and give you a memorable experience so you can never again say that you don't remember me."

That is an understatement. I understand the concept of imprinting better now.

Carly and Lilly made their way back from lunch and find us in the middle of the empty conference room. They pulled up two chairs to face us, and settled in to watch the Hurricane Hattie Comedy Hour. Hurricane Hattie stood behind me, pouring warm soapy water over my head and gently massaging my bruised head. It felt like heaven. I wondered if she knew how to stay clear of the head wound, but it was completely numb, so I guess it really didn't matter. I didn't care about much, other than wanting this shampoo to last forever.

Later, Cameron and I will have a private little joke about how I went from being an air-head with the swooshing sounds of a post-surgical bubble to a numb skull feeling no pain or sensation at all.

I introduce everybody and then Hurricane Hattie launches into her comedy routine. Once she learns Carly and Lilly are from San Francisco, she has her topic. Hurricane Hattie used to live in the bay area but moved to Arizona because she couldn't afford California housing. She directs her shtick to Carly and Lilly, her main audience.

"How do you afford living in San Francisco? Do you live in a tent or something?"

She tells a story about her cousin she used to live with in San Francisco, who works for Google. When she moved to Arizona, he moved into a place with six roommates, just to be able to make the rent. This is becoming one hilarious rant and my head massage feels heavenly. I hope her show goes on forever because that is how long I want the shampoo to last.

Hurricane Hattie jokes, "I said to my cousin, dude, you a grown ass man, why do you want to sleep on a bunkbed with a bunch of other sorry ass men?"

Her routine plays on and the topic stays on housing in-affordability and tech companies ruining the town for everyone. Carly and Lilly can relate. Hurricane Hattie knows her audience. I feel so lucky to have caught this act and am sorry Cameron isn't here to see it. He is missing quite a show.

Hurricane Hattie was right. I will never again forget her. In her clinical chart notes, which are rather dull compared to her live performance, she is very cutting. She describes me as "forgetful, impaired cognition with a tendency to shuffle feet."

She went on, "Presents with body function limitations, decreased strength, stamina and balance." These things, according to her assessment, "limit my ability to participate in ADL's (daily living activities)." Her discharge recommendation is for me to go to a skilled nursing facility, a SNF, for ongoing skilled therapy. Ouch.

Chapter 9: Rosie's Discharge Planning

After my memorable encounter with Hurricane Hattie, I am visited by the hospital social worker to chat about discharge plans. Rosie has long, glossy black hair and stands almost 5 feet tall in her 3-inch heels. She hands me a spreadsheet of rehab and skilled nursing facilities on the insurance-approved list for me to review. Cameron and I look it over and, to our collective horror, Verde Vista Care appears in the middle of the list as an approved facility. This is the nursing home where I settled my Mom to die six years prior. At the time, I was thrilled to find her a single room that overlooked a nice patio. Her room was next to the nurse's station so she had constant access and attention. She hated it, but, as I often reminded her, I was so grateful to have found this treasure—a private room was not something easily found or afforded on her public assistance. Wabi-Sabi.

Cameron says, "There is no effing way you are going there, not on my watch."

He never used to cuss, but he does now that he is hooked up with a Jersey girl.

"Why not, it wasn't as bad as you thought it was. And it isn't as though I would be in my mother's room. I would go to the newer renovated rehab wing which was much nicer than the long-term care side. Plus, Camp Verde would be geographically convenient for you to visit me."

The more I thought about it, the creepier it felt to think I could go back to that place as a patient. It still held so many memories of visits with my mom. And of her dying there. Every weekend I would take my dog and, armed with a venti Starbucks latte, try to create space for her to make her final exit.

I had taken so many calls from the Verde Vista Care staff about the challenges of managing my mom. I took more calls from my mom about how abusive and disrespectful the staff was to her. So many difficult memories.

One time my mom called me in the middle of the night to report that the staff was trying to baptize her in the showers. What!? She had just watched a program on television that exposed a controversial ritual of a fringe group in the Mormon Church posthumously baptizing dead Jews. Apparently, this controversial group believes posthumous baptizing allows the deceased people a pathway to the afterlife. The Verde Vista Care facility was Mormon-owned at the time. Who knows, maybe it wasn't all in her wild imagination.

One evening the nursing home called to say Molly's breathing had progressed to the kind they see in the final stages of the end-of-life. I rushed over to spend the night with her. I curled up on her Lazy-Boy lounge chair and settled in for the night. She lay in her inflated hospice bed, loudly snoring, with a death rattle.

The special hospice bed installed a week earlier was also breathing, up and down, inflating and deflating, rhythmically. I think it moves like that so patients don't get bed sores. I wrapped myself up in a soft woolen brown and yellow blanket that my Mom had me get dry cleaned for her the week before. I had to promise to make sure the cleaners had her special instructions so the blanket end fringe would not fray or tangle. Yeah, Molly, of course I'll make sure to tell the cleaner those instructions. Not! Maybe I secretly wanted those threads, along with her power over me, to unravel.

When Molly was gone, I folded up the blanket, tied it up in a satin yellow ribbon and gave it to a young Native American woman, a Verde Vista Care patient who was non-ambulatory and lived in the facility as a long-term resident. I said it was a gift from Molly. She thanked me and expressed her condolences for my loss.

I gave away all of Molly's stuff to people living or working in the facility—a flat screen TV, a cute wooden dresser of drawers, her Lazy Boy lift-off recliner chair and, of course, her beloved Jazzy motorized scooter. She would have wanted me to sell her things, but the residents and staff were happy with their gifts. And it made me feel better too.

The residents knew of Molly's impending death way before I did. It's a mini culture where people hear and observe things that outsiders don't see. A week before my mother's death, one of the nursing assistants breezily passed me by in the hallway and said, "Won't be long now." How did she know? An elderly arthritic man, who I saw every day but never spoke a word to because his bent spine meant face-to-face encounters were impossible, approached me minutes after I arrived the day my mother died to say, "sorry for your loss."

As her death rattle grew louder, I turned up the volume on my classic iPod. I was listening to Carol King's memoir, *Natural Woman*. Carol King was the reader. At one point, around 4:00 in the morning, I got to a place in the book where Carol broke into a chanting of the Kaddish in Hebrew, the ancient Jewish prayer of mourning recited for the dead. I sent a text to Cameron, asking how this could possibly be happening. He must have been sleeping and I'm glad I didn't wake him.

Cameron was right. No effing way was I going to Verde Vista Care.

After hearing about the horrid report from Hurricane Hattie, I told Rosie I reviewed the list of rehab facilities and wanted to go to the Mountain Valley Rehab facility in Prescott Valley. It had a marvelous reputation. They were known for making you work extremely hard, sometimes for up to five or six hours of therapy a day. It would be hard work, but I was motivated and wanted to get better. It wouldn't be as convenient for Cameron, but I thought maybe he could stay overnight at my Prescott house.

Rosie agreed it was a good choice and arranged for an interview with a Mountain Valley representative. The representative came to my hospital room, assessed me as a good candidate and started the ball rolling on the massive paperwork required for insurance green lighting. It felt good to have a plan, even though I was anxious about how difficult it was going to be.

A few hours later, I heard the click clacking of Rosie's 3-inch heels on the bare floors of the hallway, long before she entered my room. The expression on her face said,

"You're not gonna like this."

She had reviewed all my medical charting and it turns out that everyone, with the exception of Hurricane Hattie, gave me glowing gold star reports. I was walking, talking with no apparent limitations and, basically, off-the-charts with how speedily my recovery was going. Hurricane Hattie's report was an outlier. As a discharge planner, Rosie has been in this business a long time and knows her way around it. She told me based on my medical charting, she was very doubtful my insurance company would approve a stay at the pricey in-patient rehab facility of my choice. It would cost them too much money.

I was disappointed and relieved at the same time. I had psyched myself up to kick butt and get my butt kicked for a month and make a full recovery. But I also wanted to go back home, lie on the couch, read books, watch movies, eat ice cream, nap and chill. I think Cameron was slightly relieved because he just wanted to take me home. I wasn't in my sustained place of gratitude yet so I couldn't yet see or appreciate my fabulous healing brain and how quickly it was bouncing back. Aside from the brain being the most critical place for our human identity, it is an organ that isn't fully understood. Neuroplasticity, or the brain's ability to adapt to injury and compensate for deficits is one of the most promising and interesting aspects of healing after any kind of trauma on this mysterious organ.

When my visitors arrived, I told them about the change in plans. I would not be going to rehab after all. Then I cranked up Amy Winehouse on my iPhone and we went into full hospital room karaoke, singing out "try to make me go to rehab, I said no, no, no…."

Hospital Discharge – Leaving Behind
the Emerald City as an Inpatient

May 6, 2019

The next day I got released to Cameron. When he was asked by the Mayo team if he was willing to take on my supervision, he stepped up and didn't hesitate to say yes to the job. I was grateful, but not totally comfortable. I was used to calling my own shots. Gratitude for all of these good things happening would come later. Big picture profound gratitude delayed. For now, I was happy to be free to go back to our RV life, rejoin our pets and sleep next to Cameron in our own comfy bed.

It would take several hours for the paperwork, meds and discharge instructions to be produced. I could not stop smiling and tried to stay out of the way of the neuro nursing team as they prepared "my" bed for the next patient. All medications were filled through the hospital pharmacy, so that was one less trip we needed to worry about. The Emerald City team thinks of everything.

I am leaving as a changed person in so many ways. I have a new trust, admiration, awe and gratitude for doctors, the medical world and modern medicine miracles. I don't yet fully grasp the gravity of what happened here emotionally, the magnitude of the experience or the way it will forever change me. That will happen gradually over time through gratitude practice, prayer, mindfulness practice, reading and writing. My watch and wait brain tumor treatment plan will morph over time and evolve into a spiritual practice. But I don't realize any of this yet. I am just glad to be out of the hospital, with Cameron. I have always known that his practical skills outpace my own. Over time, I will recognize that his watch and wait skills do too. I am grateful he shares my burden.

It was evening by the time I got all my signed discharge paperwork instructions, pain pills, anti-nausea drugs, anti-constipation, anti-seizure drugs and hydro-colloid dressing packets for Cameron to use to clean my head wound and protect it while my body healed. We decided to pick up comfort food for our first dinner home in Dolphin-Care. I sat in the car as Cameron went inside to pick up our order. I phoned my niece Jenn from the car.

Me: Guess where I am?

Jenn: I don't know, Mayo Clinic Cactus Healing Garden?

Me: Nope, Boston Market parking lot. Cam is picking up our pot roast, potato, veggie and cornbread dinner. We are headed back to West World, checking back into Dolphin-Care.

Jenn: Shut up! Drive-through brain surgery! In and out. Fresh ingredients! You should offer to do a Mayo Clinic commercial ...Mayo Clinic, we'll get you in for a little brain surgery on Friday morning and have you picking up your curbside takeout food on Monday night! We do it your way!

She later told me she thought I would be stuck inside a rehab hospital for weeks on end. So did I.

Before my diagnosis, Jenn was visiting me in Prescott and we were on a dog walk in my neighborhood park. Or more accurately, a dog run. Paisley was her usual outdoor-crazy-dog self, pulling me behind her, unable to contain her exuberance and joy. As she was running up and down the creek bank with me in tow, hanging onto her leash for dear life, I suddenly lost control, tripped and fell flat on my butt. I never let go of the leash.

I told Jenny about this "forward momentum" phenomenon I was experiencing, where I was unable to stop myself. I told her I thought I had Parkinson's, like my

Mom. She rolled her eyes, said, "Wipe the snot from your nose, get up, get a new harness leash, and, no, you don't have Parkinson's just because Molly did."

She can be very tough love and direct. Now that I have my definitive diagnosis, I love giving her shit.

"Hey, I have a brain tumor, Jenny."

"Oh, gimme a break. I will be visiting you in your Jewish assisted living when you're ninety-eight years old and you'll be shouting, 'Jenny, I have a brain tumor, now move out of the way of my TV screen so I can watch my favorite Kathy Powers show.'"

She knows it's Rachel Maddow, but she likes to make up funny stuff to keep me laughing.

PART II

Not Knowing

CHAPTER 10: NEXT: THE HUNT FOR ASSISTED, INDEPENDENT OR HYBRID LIVING

Though he wasn't saying a lot, I could tell Cameron thought assisted living was a bad idea. He thought I should live with him and recover independently. He questioned my desire and judgment about moving to a place he called "an old folks' home." No amount of correcting him on this dated phrase would change or open his mind, but he agreed to drive me around to look at a few places. I didn't trust myself to live independently in my own place yet. I wanted to see my options in person. It was time to find out what came next in the after the BS "new normal."

I didn't trust my brain or my balance. Even though I didn't feel confident to live on my own, I was concerned about being a burden on Cameron. My balance was still wobbly and my short-term memory wasn't functioning very well. I remember thanking G-d and my brilliant neurosurgery team that I was no longer wet. I was over the moon that my bladder was working fine and finally had the confidence to give up the "discreet undergarments."

Before we visited assisted facilities, and wanting to keep all options open, Cameron installed grab bars and handrails on my steep and narrow Prescott house steps leading to the garage where I did my laundry and parked my car. Once the safety accommodations were installed, I tested them out.

I tried to show confidence, pretending how easily I could navigate those steep and scary steps. Neither of us totally trusted my balance. It bothered me thinking about how I used to run up and down those steps, hands-free, several times a day. Cameron wasn't buying my feigned confidence and threatened to nail the door shut if I continued to navigate the creaky old stairs on my own. I looked around to see what kind of accommodations we could make to the house to give me more security. The only real challenge in the daily living activities was the laundry. The washer and dryer were in the garage and there were only two ways down. One way was an inside steep stairwell, dangerous even with the newly installed grab bars. The other was an outdoor set of steps that weren't as steep, but were narrow and uneven.

I had visions of our veterinarian who, many years ago, came to the house to put my beloved eighty-pound puppy Kaizen to sleep because she had a heart tumor. He saw the uneven steps and, while cradling my girl in his arms said, "G-d, I hope I don't wipe out on these steps." I walked behind to steady him and opened up the passenger side of the cab of his truck. He just looked at me with a pained and apologetic expression and told me he would be laying Kaizen on a blanket in the back of the open truck bed. I stood there for a long time, petting Kaizen's stiff body while tears dropped onto her fur. I expected him to place her inside the cab, next to him, and was disappointed she would be alone in the back of a pickup truck.

Suddenly my broken brain had a brainstorm. I could move the washer and dryer up to the first floor and put them in a back bedroom or a pantry. Brilliant, the new normal was emerging as one-level living. Life was getting smaller, but it was also getting simpler. When I told my neighbor about the plan, he lit a fire under me by saying I better hurry up if I was going to buy a new and smaller washer and dryer because the occupant in the White House was about to mess with tariffs and imports and everything coming up from Mexico was going to rise in price.

That afternoon, Cameron took measurements and we decided the pantry would be the prime spot because it would require the least amount of plumbing retrofitting.

I went online with my credit card in hand, ready to place my order. The brain surgery hadn't wiped out my impulsivity. Since Cameron was now technically my supervisor, he overrode the impulse order and insisted we at least take a trip to a big box store and actually look at the machines.

As we walked into Best Buy, my overstimulated brain went into flooding mode from all the lights and noise. It felt like walking into a giant MRI machine. I managed to look at the few washer and dryer models we had seen online, the ones that would fit inside the pantry. They would be fine. I made a mad dash out of the store. We went home, I sat down on the couch, pulled out my credit card and placed the order for the exact machines I was going to impulse buy a few hours earlier. Note to self: Stay out of big box stores for now and trust your impulsive intuition.

With my post-surgical vision deficits, I still wasn't confident that I could reverse the car out of the garage without sideswiping the walls and adding to the growing collection of dings and dents. The side of my car is worn, just like my skull. I reassured myself and Cameron that I could always park the car in the driveway, but I was secretly petrified to get behind the wheel. I installed an Uber app on my phone and decided to wait until I completed an occupational therapy program and got professionally cleared before attempting to drive again.

Simplifying down to one-level-living was working in a few different ways, not just home alterations. My world had to get smaller in order to build my confidence back up to my independent life. But I wasn't there yet. Moving back home seemed like a physical possibility, but I neglected to consider my new emotional needs. The new washer and dryer were great and the one floor living space fantastic, but I didn't want to be alone. I was happy as long as I had the security of Cameron staying with me overnight and driving me wherever I needed to go. I thought this growing dependence on him might ruin our relationship and that was the most important thing to me.

I convinced a very reluctant and resistant Cameron to drive me around to check out a few senior living complexes that might provide me with the security I needed to adjust to the new normal. For some reason, I hate this overused term of "new normal" and can't believe I am using it here. Hopefully, it will get edited out.

The next few days were spent driving around and looking at assisted and independent living apartments, two in Prescott and one in Sedona. Cameron accompanied me inside the two Prescott facilities. We stopped at the lobby desk and checked in with a woman seated behind a large granite-topped desk. She asked if we had an appointment. No, we didn't know we needed one and said we just wanted to have a look around the lobby area. She eyed us suspiciously, handed us a business card for the marketing rep who would not be back until the following day. We thanked her and wandered further into the area of public couches and overstuffed chairs. She got up and followed us around as if we were potential shoplifters in a department store.

There was an elderly woman sitting alone at a table for four in the empty café dining area. She had a cup of coffee and was picking at the crust on a piece of cherry pie. She was all dressed up in a tweed jacket, a calf length woolen skirt with nylon stockings and orthopedic shoes. A bright multi-colored decorative cane leaned up against the empty chair next to her. She was wearing makeup and colorful chunky jewelry. Her floral-patterned oversized handbag was draped across the back of her chair. She looked like somebody's sweet grandmother, nostalgic for a life she used to lead and a little desperate for a bit of conversation. She said hello to us and we asked if she minded if we joined her. She said she would be delighted.

We told her we were looking around because I was considering a possible move into one of the independent apartments and we asked her if she enjoyed living there.

"The food is very good and there is usually fresh coffee in the lobby. They keep the place clean. And they have activities day and night, but I don't go to many events. I mostly keep to myself. It was a difficult adjustment moving here after keeping house for more than sixty years." She mentioned her hometown, somewhere in the Midwest. "After my husband died two years ago, my children didn't think I could manage the upkeep on my house. They said it was too much for me and they always worried about my safety. But I miss my house. After all, I was there for sixty years. It's nice here, but it isn't like my own house and all my things. At least my children are not worrying now, but I miss home."

She had a sadness and a resilience about her that made her conversation sad and sweet. When she finally took a bite of her pie, Cameron and I looked at each other and knew this was our exit opportunity. We thanked her for chatting with us. She said the pleasure was all hers and to come back any time to visit. She said we should come at meal time so we could sample the food while we visited. I got the sense she was lonely and starved for conversation. I wondered if her children visited her. I was starting to question whether senior living was for me. Trading independence for security, it suddenly didn't seem all that.

The next place was much fancier and marketed as a holistic lifestyle. High noon organic teas were served in the café, massages and mindfulness programs were available to residents, along with weekly housecleaning and shopping trips. My ears perked up hearing about the housekeeping. Cameron rolled his eyes.

"Let's try to keep an open mind," I said.

We checked in at the fancy reception desk and were advised our tour guide was running a bit late. This time we knew we needed an appointment. We were invited to have a cup of fresh organic tea in the beautifully decorated lobby cafe. We headed over and each of us grabbed a complimentary newspaper. Cameron turned down the tea, but I poured myself a cup and picked up a small plate with two butter cookies and a thin slice of coffee cake. I remember being disappointed the high tea was an ordinary box of assorted herbal teabags and the coffee cake looked like a familiar Safeway bakery product. Not quite as good as the pictures in the brochure, but I was getting more and more cynical as this adventure tour continued. None of the brochures listed move-in costs or monthly prices.

When we finished reading the paper, our guide still had not showed up. I looked at Cameron and said, "Let's leave and reschedule." He was out of his overstuffed plush upholstered chair in under two seconds.

Three days later we headed back over the mountain to Cameron's house, together. We found a big and expensive box of beautiful flowers on the doorstep. I assumed it was a get-well gift from one of my relatives back east, but it was from the marketing director of the assisted living place where we missed the tour. Cameron said,

"See why they don't publish their prices. This is what you'd be paying for."

I had no idea how I would afford assisted housing. I supposed I would sell my house and that would probably last about five or six years.

I opened the box of flowers which I was sure was at least a $50 bouquet. It had been sitting on the doorstep for several days in the heat while we were in Prescott, so the gorgeous bouquet was a bit wilted. What a perfect metaphor.

The next day Cameron drove me to the third assisted living place in Sedona. This time he refused to get out of the car. I could tell he was running out of patience for this "old folks' home" visiting activity.

The director greeted me and gave me a tour of an apartment that was recently vacated and being painted and prepped for a new resident. It was a mess, with clothing and personal effects strewn all over. She shuffled me out of the apartment, embarrassed, explaining the apartment was being used as temporary housing by the construction workers until the renovation was completed. She steered me to her cozy office and offered me a cup of tea. I declined, knowing Cameron was waiting in the parking lot.

This place also included weekly house cleaning, but no fancy coffees or mindfulness classes. The director wanted me to know I would be most welcome, but also wanted me to understand I would have been the youngest resident by about twenty-five years. I thanked her and walked away without looking back.

As I got in the car, I guess I wanted reassurance that I wasn't a burden. I knew Cameron was opposed to any of the assisted living places, but tried to stay quiet with his opinion. I knew he wanted to take me home and take care of me. He wanted to keep me close. He was becoming overprotective and I was becoming overly dependent. I worried about all of this and of being a burden. I still worry about it today.

I didn't think I could live at Cameron's house because of his "collector" tendencies. I knew he couldn't move into my minimalist cabin in the woods without all the comfort of his stuff around him. I was too tired to make any decisions. I needed to nap. The neuro fatigue, a very special kind of tiredness, was kicking in. Ten seconds after walking through the door to Cameron's house, I dropped onto the couch. Just before falling into a deep and healing neuro-fatigue sleep, I remember calling out to him,

"Am I a burden?"

He answered as he was walking out of the room and I wasn't sure I heard him properly, but was too tired to ask for clarity. What I thought I heard him say, "You're not a bird on an island."

Did he mean that metaphorically about independence vs. connection and needing his help? Or was I overthinking things as usual and just not hearing him right. Then I fell into a deep and luxurious brain-recovery sleep.

When I awoke, I was alone in the house. I called out for Cameron. No answer. I got to my feet and opened the garage door. I counted the cars. The Opel GT and the classic AMC he was restoring were both in their spots. I went out to the driveway and counted off the other cars on my fingers. They all seemed to be there. Cameron has too many cars. I suddenly panicked. My imagination went wild. Thoughts went racing through my head, "He's left me. I knew he would. I can't blame him. I am a burden. He has had enough. What will I do now? I need to move into an assisted living place right away. I'm scared."

My phone rang. It was him. He said he was on a quick errand, driving one of the six or seven cars that I had forgotten. He hadn't wanted to wake me up just to say he was popping out for an errand. He was on his way home. I started to breathe normally again.

I have been living in Cameron's house for a little over a year now and I happily walk around the clutter. Even in the dark. When I go out to the backyard to do a skunk check before letting Paisley out to pee, I step over a recently used weed eater carelessly tossed across the passageway, lying on its side where it was dropped earlier in the day. I smile, grateful to have remembered it is there and for the ability to step over it without losing my balance.

Clutter seems like small stuff to me now and I work around it. I have one corner in the bedroom where my clothes live inside the laundry basket I used to carry back and forth on weekends. There are no extra dresser drawers for me and when Cameron suggests moving his clothing out of one to free it up for me, I don't want it. I am happy with my laundry basket and bags. I am happy with my wabi-sabi transient life.

I put a cover on the stained leather couch to hide the blemishes and think about my new calming philosophy of wabi-sabi. I go beyond the brain metaphor and apply the philosophy as aesthetic to the house and yard. If I'm not exactly finding beauty, I am accepting peacefully and gratefully and letting go of the idea of organizing things here. My desire to share this life together is the priority. I can't change everything to be clean and clutter-free, the way I think it should be. But I can appreciate the way it is.

The dust bunnies in the house abound. The floors always need vacuuming. There are handprints near the front door walls where I lean to balance while taking off my shoes. The kitchen counter tops are permanently stained and the tables have piles of papers and mail, but the home-brewed coffee, served up in bed, is always amazing.

CHAPTER 11: LIFE AS AN OUTPATIENT AND A RETURN TO THE MARVELOUS MAYO

May 15, 2019

I am expecting to meet with Dr. Porter for the first post-surgical follow-up. Cameron and I are both excited about showing her my marked improvements. My bladder problems are completely resolved, I am thinking pretty clearly and my balance is improving every day. The consulting room door opens and a lovely, younger woman walks in, extends her hand and introduces herself.

"Hi! I am Dr. Sharma. I've read your file. You are now post-surgical for pineal mass and hydrocephalus and you look fantastic."

Cameron says, "Oh, you should have seen her before. She was in bad shape. Now she has her expression back, her brightness is here and she is interactive again. She is amazing now compared to how she was before."

Dr. Sharma smiles. She exudes great positive energy and explains she is Dr. Porter's student. She proudly tells us she graduated from medical school on this very day. We congratulate her and I tell her she is now and will be a fabulous doctor. She is so personable. She asks permission to do a neuro assessment.

"Of course," here we go again. Same 'ol, same 'ol.

"Squeeze my hand, touch your nose, touch my finger, tap your feet, close your eyes."

Dr. Sharma hikes her skirt up and moves in close to me. Her skin-tight silky supportive undergarments are on clear display and she clearly does not care. She is focused only on her patient, me. She speaks very encouragingly about my plan to begin outpatient occupational therapy soon, since that will help my recovery from what she calls "neurological sequelae of hydrocephalus." I make a note to look up the word *sequelae* later.

> **"Sequelae**: a condition which is the consequence of a **previous** disease or injury."

I love the emphasis on the word ***previous.***

Dr. Sharma writes out a new prescription for a different form of Zofran for the post-surgical nausea. I already have a Zofran prescription, but it was too strong and was actually making me sicker. She explained the form she was prescribing is a timed-release smaller dose formula that should work better. Fortunately, it does. I start to refer to the new Zofran as my Zofriend.

Although I thoroughly enjoyed meeting Dr. Sharma, I am disappointed not to be meeting with Dr. Porter. I have prepared and am ready for her this time. I know what year it is and I have practiced drawing the 3-D cube. I think I will be able to copy the image today. The consult room door opens slightly and Dr. Porter peeks in. She doesn't see a wheel chair.

"Ah, you are walking on your own?"

She then pushes the door to open wider and it crashes into my cherry red Rollater walker. I am getting around well with the walker, but not yet able to walk on my own without the support. At Cameron's, I am preparing for my upcoming occupational therapy by doing morning laps around the community tennis courts. I can do three or four laps before having to sit and rest.

I am competing against a ninety-five-year-old neighbor named Ace. He does thirty laps every day. It is no competition. He tells me he has been at it for at least five years and encourages me to keep going. I will soon be able to leave behind the Rollater and get back to walking Paisley on my own two feet. When I stop by the tennis courts to show off my progress, Ace says,

"I may have to go in and get a little brain surgery if those are the results you get."

Dr. Porter is very warm and friendly today. We can tell she is proud of her newly graduated student and pleased with her mentee's doctor skills. She sits down and says, "Let's do a little assessment."

Today I am ready.

"Okay, I know what year it is and I may even be able to calculate some numbers and recall a list of words."

"Yeah, we're not going to do any of that today. Why don't you just tell me what has happened to you since our last meeting."

I wonder if Dr. Porter realizes she just asked me the single question that will trigger my desire to understand what happened to me and plant the seed for my true moment of awakening. With this one question, she started me on the road to full recovery.

"Okay, I've had surgery to fix my hydrocephalus and had an Ommaya reservoir implanted as a bypass around the tumor that was blocking my cerebral spinal fluid flow."

She nods, looking pleased. She adds to my answer. "And you had an ETV, which is how the hydrocephalus got resolved."

I had forgotten the name of the procedure. I tell her about my experience waking up to Dr. Devi 'Twill-resolve thanking me. I said I was confused and in awe that he was thanking me after he had just saved my life.

"That is because our work is built on trust and we could not do what we do without that trust. He was thanking you for the trust."

I am beginning to trust Dr. Porter. We are connecting. I am appreciating her honesty and directness. She tells me the sampling of the cerebral spinal fluid obtained during surgery did not demonstrate any abnormal cells and she is somewhat reassured by the benign nature of it. The mass does not appear to be a germinoma and the fact that the tumor has so many calcifications suggest that it is slow growing. She is encouraged by my improvements and explains two options going forward. "Option one: Go back in for a biopsy immediately. Option two: Continue recovering, regularly monitor the mass on MRIs and only intervene if it grows."

Excuse the pun, but it's a no-brainer. I look over at Cameron for a nano-second and tell Dr. Porter my preference is for the latter. She says that would be her preference too. I start to cry. Cameron starts to tear up (not a common sight) and Dr. Porter hands both of us a tissue. She seems moved and softened. I am now seeing the absolute beauty in her realistic, no-nonsense approach. In this moment, Dr. Porter becomes my new hero. I trust her implicitly and know now that she is my advocate.

The next day I have a follow-up meeting in the Neurosurgery basement wing of the Emerald City with Dr. Kintsugi aka Bernie or The Boss. I have come for a blessing of the pineal mass, known to me, my family and friends by the name of Pinena. I have not had the nerve to share the tumor naming with the neurodocs yet.

If Pinena had come to me before choosing to go rogue and divide uncontrollably into a bunch of silly cells, I would not have offered her a blessing. Yet, I want one from Bernie.

Dr. Kintsugi is running two hours late. We have a lot of time to think. I wonder why the neurosurgery department is housed in the basement when the work they do is focused on the top floor of the body, the brains. When Bernie enters the conference room, wearing full scrubs, he apologizes for his lateness, obviously stressed by the way his day was going. He is normally exceptionally calm. When a neurosurgeon is having a bad day, it isn't like Starbucks messing up your morning latte order.

I want him to see how wonderfully I am healing and how much progress I am making in my recovery. He seems to want to cut to the surgical chase today and begins talking about the different angles he can re-enter my brain to reach the pineal mass that eluded him on his last visit. Normally, I am completely deferential. Not today.

The Jersey Girl attitude emerges and wants to shout out,

"Whoa, dude, slow your roll."

Instead, I assertively but politely interrupt and remind him since the tumor showed no growth on the scans, the decision to go with a WaWa option was the plan made with Dr. Porter a few days earlier.

In hindsight, I realize he probably had not even had time to read Dr. Porter's notes and wasn't aware of the plan. Now that he hears it, he is willing to go along and dictates his electronic notes

"Patient wishes to take the more conservative path. We will schedule a Spectroscopy MRI in ten weeks."

He explained the specialized spectroscopy MRI would analyze the chemical composition of the tumor and compare it to other brain tissue. This might give us more information about the pathology. He then issued the following doctor's orders:

"Go, relax and celebrate your new health. Continue to heal. Take a vacation."

After hearing these orders, I ask if he would bless my tumor. I could feel Cameron cringe and watch as he buries his head in his hands with embarrassment. I look deeply into Dr. Kintsugi's eyes with profound gratitude.

He deadpans, "You're blessed."

I wonder if he may have been thinking to himself, *Oh yeah, these are my patients from up north in Sedona. Crystal Country.* Later I will title this episode #Blessingofthetumor when I send out the journal entries to my supporters. Much later, I will share the journal entry with a fellow writing student and she will tell me the hashtag will be confusing to older readers. She will also tell me that using the phrase "old folks' home" when writing about assisted living facilities is ageist and older readers will find it offensive. She didn't say she was offended, but maybe she was.

Cameron, Dr. Kintsugi and I stand up together and head down the corridor. Before reaching the lobby, Dr. Kintsugi motions for us to enter the inner sanctum of the neuro work-room. He wants to show us something.

There on a shelf, above the bank of big computer monitors, sits a tiny gift enclosure tag. He kept it from the box of See's Candy, the gratitude chocolate gift, I had delivered to his office after surgery. At the time, Cameron thought chocolates was a dumb idea. I disagreed.

"No, it's a great idea. What else would you get someone who just saved your life? Why, chocolate, of course." And a ritual is born. Neurodocs will be getting boxes of gratitude chocolates for as long as we share this WaWa life plan together.

I leaned over to see the gift tag sitting on the shelf and squinted to read the note, recognizing my own tiny scrawled handwriting. "To Dr. B and his awesome team. Thank you for giving me back my life." I signed my first name and drew a little heart.

Our go-forward plans may have been different, but if you listen hard and pay close attention, you can hear and see the profound gratitude and trust we share.

A year later, on reflection and through the memoir writing experience, it has become clear that we were operating under different assumptions and beliefs at that first post-op meeting. There were always two plans in play, his and mine.

In our very first meeting, Dr. Kintsugi explained the risks of the ETV surgery and Ommaya reservoir placement to us which included stroke, hemorrhage, infection, failure of procedure and a few other medical and neurological complications. Risk of serious complications are guessed at 5%. He warned us of the possibility of a shunt implant if the 3rd ventriculostomy failed to work.

He said he would bring me back at a later date for an open biopsy if he wasn't able to reach it during the ETV surgery, but neither Cameron or I heard this part. This back up plan was clearly stated in the written report and when I read the report one year later, it all made perfect sense.

CHAPTER 12: OCCUPATIONAL THERAPY KVETCH

I spent the whole month of July in outpatient occupational therapy in Sedona, Ironically, it is the same rehab facility that would not accept me into the *Big and Loud* class for Parkinson's disease patients because I couldn't produce the required doctor's diagnosis. I was self-misdiagnosed at that time.

Cameron drives me to my first session and it feels like the first day of school. Instead of dropping me off in the parking lot, he walks me into the lobby and says he will stay just long enough to meet my therapist, like a parent would want to meet the kindergarten teacher on the first day of school. When he picks me up at the end of the session, he has a little packet of my favorite oatmeal cookies he picked up from a McDonald's drive through run.

Today I am here to work on my post-op visual perception deficits so I can be cleared to start driving again. My therapy goal is to reduce the amount of time it takes between physically seeing things and my brain understanding what to do with that visual information. I need to close the gap so I am safe and feel confident to drive again.

I spend loads of time on puzzle work, matching up different images, drawing and copying patterns, picking out dissimilar objects and doing jigsaw puzzles, upside down.

One day, my therapist Mark is running late. He sets a mound of Playdoh in front of me and tells me to find and pull out the eight glass marbles embedded in the blue and white swirly blob. As I stick my hands inside, feeling around for the marbles, I wonder how many other hands have been there and worry about the germs and microbes left behind. I am certain Playdoh would not be therapy protocol in Covid-19 times. I wanted to sing out, "wash your hands, wash your hands, wash your hands" well before the deadly virus arrived and we all went into frequent pandemic hand-washing mode. Even back then it felt like a Petri dish for germs. I hated the feeling of the well-used Playdoh getting embedded underneath my fingernails.

A few feet away, a young Black woman is massaging an elderly white woman's hands. We were never officially introduced, but we sat together in an open-space treatment area for weeks and connected in a quiet way. Her patients usually go into a blissful place as she manipulates their arthritic hands, just the way I did when my Emerald City occupational therapist Hurricane Hattie massaged and shampooed my head. I never learned this woman's name, but I never forgot her either. She radiated so much body positivity in a plus-size way and exuded a warm and compassionate energy. As we chatted, I learned she was working toward her degree in Physical Therapy at a university in Chicago and was here in Sedona on a summer internship.

I wondered how she felt working in this environment and was curious if she felt comfortable or uncomfortable as the only Black person in a completely white environment. Did she feel a racial difference? Now I wonder why I didn't follow up on my curiosity and ask her about it. The patient demographic in this place is 99.9% old and white (me included). The therapist demographic is 100% young, fit and white. She was young, but not white or particularly fit.

When we first met, I was the first to speak. I pointed to the hand massage she was giving her elderly patient.

"Why can't my therapist Mark do that?"

I thought she was giving her patient a manicure. We laughed together and our quiet connection was made. I bonded with her more than anyone else in the place, including my own therapist and his assistant. So why didn't I follow my curiosity and ask her what it was like for her as a Black woman, and a student, to be working in this old and white environment? I should have asked her that question, even if it made me uncomfortable, because I was truly curious. She was a Black life that mattered a lot to me. I felt comforted by our connection and her presence. Knowing she would be there made therapy more enjoyable and I wish I had told her that.

My therapist Mark entered the open room with a stack of paper puzzles. He sat across the table from me, placed a card with an image of a three-dimensional cube in front of me and instructed me to copy the image.

"Noooooo! Puuhhhlease, Maaaaarrrrrk, not the three-dimensional cube."

This was triggering flashbacks to the trauma of not being able to do this task in one of my neuro evaluations with Dr. Porter. It was particularly frustrating because I can remember easily drawing this cube, just for fun, as an eight-year-old child. I turned to my student therapist friend and said with pride,

"I'm a complainer."

"Hey, at least you own it, Sister."

We laughed and I realize now how proud I was to be a complainer. In Jewish, we call this kvetching and consider it a bit of an art form. And it worked for me. Mark put the three-dimensional card back in the pack and presented me with a different image to draw.

Today I take pride in choosing not to be a complainer. It no longer suits me. I prefer to live in gratitude and the two are not compatible. You cannot live in gratitude and complain at the same time. It is just simply impossible.

The following week, Mark administered a final test to see if my visual perception deficits had improved enough for me to be discharged. I had been here twice weekly for a full month and my insurance benefits were about to run out. After he graphed out my answers from rounds and rounds of matching up different but similar images, he pronounced me "Normal." Well, at least according to the chart, I was within the normal range for visual perception. I turned to my friend at the next table and asked,

"Did you hear that? I'm normal."

"Yeah, I heard." She shook her head and smiled.

That evening I was the last patient and the therapists were scrambling to close up and get home. I was standing in the parking lot, waiting for Cameron to pick me up. Two of the very white, young and fit therapists blew right past me in the parking lot without saying a word. One hopped into her gleaming white SUV and the other into his shiny blue expensive looking sports car. There was no good night greeting or have a nice evening. I was invisible to them. Their work day was over.

As the intern and lowest person on the totem pole, my friend was tasked with locking up so she was the last one to exit the building. When she saw me standing there, she asked if I needed a ride. I thanked her and told her I would be getting picked up soon. We told each other to have a great night. She got into her old beater car and headed out to make the long trek over the mountain to Prescott. I think she was staying there with friends during her summer internship.

CHAPTER 13: SCANXIETY

"Scanxiety: (n) Anxiety and worry that accompanies the period of time leading up to an MRI and the time between undergoing the scan and receiving the results."

The scanxiety she felt as she awaited the results of her MRI felt akin to putting her head back on the chopping block.

The entry underneath *Scanxiety* in *The Urban Dictionary* is:

"Brain Bleach: (n) "brān blēch": Man's greatest invention, brain bleach removes bad memories and general "Do Not Want" moments. Every household should have a few gallons."

You have a brain tumor, have some Brain Bleach.

In Act 2 of this story, I have developed a case of Scanxiety. There's a difference between general anxiety and scanxiety. I learned about this difference in one of my brainpeep groups, the fellow survivors who understand. It's not as much worrying about what might happen. It's more about remembering what has already happened. It's about remembering the first time my world was rocked with five fateful words – you have a brain tumor. It's about remembering the horror of being wet, wobbly and wacky.

My world hasn't rocked back to center yet. I am just learning how to keep my balance on the Tilt-A-Whirl ride. The good news is, with each quarterly scan my memory continues to improve. The bad news is, because I now remember, the scanxiety also builds.

Scanxiety brings a frenzied cerebral energy along with a desperate search to find peace of mind. I am always waiting for the other shoe to drop. In all honesty, it is the nature of my personality to always expect the worst. By taking the deep dive into the WaWa world, I gave myself a powerful insight. It's as if I said to myself, "I've got news for you (me), the other shoe has already dropped and you (I) have survived." But I don't fully understand this yet.

I jump around frenetically from source to source, exploring Jewish mysticism and Buddhist wisdom to try to calm myself down, especially as each new scan approaches.

It won't be until Act 3 of this story that I will move beyond trying to buy my way out with spiritual book purchases, classes and voracious reading. That's the easy way. The hard way is the actual practice and that is the only way I will learn to turn a wabi-sabi philosophy into a personal lifestyle.

In addition to the ruminating over things that happened in the past, urine streaming down my leg while out on a dog walk, forgetting where I parked the car or tripping up the stairs, scanxiety is about the "what if" thoughts of the future too. *"What if Pinena grows? What if Bernie recommends a new protocol of tumor removal? What if Dr. Porter thinks radiation is warranted? What will I say or do? So far, they have been open and willing partners and leave treatment decisions to me, but will it always be that way?"*

Making Peace with Gadolinium, Scanxiety's Companion

Every MRI includes a shot of intravenous contrast dye called Gadolinium. I am told this is the agent that "lights up" the tumor girls to make it easier to see just what they are up to. Sometimes I picture the MRI technician dressed up in police uniform, needle in hand, approaching the table and speaking to Pinena:

"You know why I'm lighting you up, Ma'am? I am giving you a caution today; Do Not Grow. Here's your warning ticket, now have a nice ride."

One of my brainpeep Facebook groups posted an article about Chuck Norris suing the health companies for $10 million. He believes the toxicity of Gadolinium poisoned his wife through her MRI's. The article mentions Mayo Clinic research on the toxicity and dangers of the drug. So why am I getting injected with this stuff, at my Mayo Clinic scans?

At my next meeting, I bring it up with Dr. Porter.

"Can I can forego the Gadolinium during the MRI's and do the scans without contrast?"

"No," is her answer, in true, inimitable Dr. Porter style. Then she asks me about my concerns and I tell her about the Chuck Norris article.

"And that is why social media can be a good and a bad thing."

She went on to tell me the enhancement provided by the Gadolinium is critical to see exactly what is going on with Pinena. Only she doesn't know her name, so she just calls her "the tumor." Once again, no mention of Li'l Miss Pollyanna, just a little schwannoma. She tells me Mayo uses a water-soluble form of the drug that flushes out of the system in a few days and reminds me to drink lots of fluids after each scan. It is only potentially a problem if there is an allergic reaction or if kidney function is compromised. So far, I don't have either of those problems. Thank you.

My obsessive mind decides to Google the poison. Wikipedia tells me Gadolinium is "a chemical element with the symbol Gd and atomic element number 64. Wait, what? When I was growing up, I was taught in Hebrew School to write the name of G-d as G-d. It is Jewish custom to substitute the middle letter "O" with a dash or eliminate it altogether because this symbolizes the ultimate awe, reverence and respect for Hashem, a Hebrew word that translates to "the Name." The Name is too sacred to be spoken. Some Jews believe any documents containing the Name Hashem become holy and should never be destroyed, erased or crossed out. These days, it is more likely to be overwritten or lost in cyberspace.

Living wabi-sabi on the WaWa is a state of mind and Gd 64, like everything else, fits inside this plan. It's the balance between putting forth effort by doing my research and then letting go. I try to remember this as I get pulled out of the MRI machine and injected with the horrid Gad. I remind myself to drink lots of fluid after the ride and choose to trust. It is the right thing to do. I modify the recovery slogan of Let Go and Let G-d to include another name that *can* be written. Let Go, Let G-d and Let Dr. Porter.

PART III

Post-Traumatic Spiritual Growth (PTSG)

CHAPTER 14: GRATITUDE

"Faced with demoralization, gratitude has the power to energize. Faced with brokenness, gratitude has the power to heal. Faced with despair, gratitude has the power to bring hope."
–Robert Emmon

"Thankfulness is modern day alchemy; it can yield happiness, grace and peace beyond imagination."
– Anonymous

Post Traumatic Spiritual Growth (PTSG) is when positive life changes develop as a result of a stressful, frightening experience. It is different from resilience. Resilience describes people "bouncing back" or returning to their previous levels of functioning. PTSG is better, it takes you to a place where you want to do better. Here I go self-diagnosing again, but I'm pretty certain I've got a good case of PTSG. I want to do better. And through a practice of gratitude, I believe I can.

If I could write a book called *How to Dial Down Your Scanxiety from a 10 to a 2*, then I might just have a best-selling memoir. But it wouldn't need to be told in a full-length memoir. My six-word memoir: Cultivate Gratitude,

Take Nothing for Granted. Sounds cliched, but this practice and way of life has transformed me. It is the prescription. Period. Full stop. Or as the Jewish elders say, the rest is commentary.

I have found it to be a simple but not easy answer. Navigating gratefulness and taking nothing for granted while living life with a couple of brain tumors takes a lot of practice. It takes trusting it in the midst of scanxiety, being present and seeing what is true and beautiful in the moment. Committing to a daily discipline of practicing gratitude takes a big will.

As I write this sentence a lightbulb goes on in my brain. Finally, the interpretation of my Thanksgiving Day *Big Will* dream emerges. Last Thanksgiving, I had a very vivid dream. I knew it was an important one, but wasn't sure what it meant. In the dream, I saw block letters, spelling out two words, "Big," and "Will," centered on a bright hot pink background. That was the whole dream.

The Big Will Dream

It's a clear, crisp Thanksgiving afternoon and I am sitting around the living room, surrounded by family guests. We are chatting and munching from plates of deviled eggs, cheese and crackers and bowls of chips and salsa. Delicious cooking smells of black lentil casserole, mashed potatoes and green beans are wafting through the house. Our holiday chefs, Carly and Lilly, are mostly vegetarian. We've prepared a piece of salmon and mushy broccoli for Lester, Cameron's elderly dad.

I share the dream I had the night before, curious to hear interpretations. Lester had a quick and literal read:

"Maybe you're coming into a large inheritance."

"Why," I joked, "are you changing your will to include me?"

Carly and Lilly are both therapists and their answer reflects their profession.

"Well, what do you think it means?"

Somebody questioned the color pink and remarked how it has become synonymous with breast cancer awareness. Out of the blue, Carly asked,

"If you had to have another brain surgery, would you do it?"

"I'm not sure," I whisper, not wanting Cameron to hear my answer.

Some discussion around the will to live as a possible dream interpretation followed this awkward exchange. I knew I was sitting among my loving family of atheists, so I didn't share my thoughts and musings around G-d's will.

The dictionary definition states:

> "Will is a desire, purpose or intention. A mental faculty by which one deliberately chooses or decides upon a course of action."

The Hebrew word for will and desire is *Ratzon*. The Kabbalists explain, "*Ratzon* is the most powerful force within the human being and awakening the desire to understand will is a way to awaken the heart and mind."

I put the heady stuff aside for a later contemplation and sat down to enjoy a lovely Thanksgiving family meal.

Nine months later, I now understand the unforgettable dream's message. It's about having the will to train my mind, with practice, to think gratefully and cultivate a daily practice and discipline of gratitude. Willpower is what the Big Will dream means to me. It fits both aspects of the definition of a dream, the image that came to my mind during sleep and a cherished aspiration, ambition and ideal. My dream and aspiration are to cultivate a gratitude practice in the midst of the inevitable health challenges that are a natural part of life, no matter what.

Pollyanna says, gratitude is always the answer. She is one of the wisest teachers I've met along the way and it turns out she was inside me the whole time. Li'l Miss Pollyanna, the small but mighty schwannoma, a tangible reminder who says gratitude is the best way to start, finish, live each and every day and experience an energetic shift by making this choice.

Posthumous Addytood of Graddytood Cawfee Talk with My Mother Molly, in the Ether, May 2020

Daughter: I thought I could neatly pack you inside of one chapter, Molly. It turns out you are too large to contain. Your ripples keep spreading out everywhere. Let's have cawfee, just you, me and Pollyanna. You haven't met her yet, but I think you might like her. Her name means gratitude. You probably read her story as a little girl. I'd like to have her here as a shield, a protection against the pain, anguish and frustration I used to feel in your presence. I am different now. And a big part of how I am different is thanks (no pun intended) to her. So, can we just sit for a while and share a cuppa?

Mother: Yes, I read the Pollyanna story as a little girl, but what's her relationship to you? Another one of the many people with problems who always somehow find you?

Daughter: No, she is my small but mighty brain tumor.

Mother: What, you have a brain tumor? And you gave her a name? Oy vey, you've gone completely meshuggeneh since I left you.

Daughter: I would like to set some cawfee tawk boundaries here, OK, Mom? Let's lay out some ground rules. You and I can ask any questions we like, but Pollyanna will be giving us all the answers.

Mother: Why?

Daughter: Because gratitude is always the answer.

Mother: Oy vey. Do what you want. I don't care. Is this Pollyanna of yours Jewish?

Daughter: Of course, she lives in my head. Remember when you used to tell me in your thick Philly accent how you didn't like my *Addytood*?

Mother: That was a long time ago. But, yes, you seemed to be moving backward rather than forward in your life, if I recall.

Daughter: Well now I've found an *Addytood of Graddytood*. I'm not sure if you would consider this moving forward, but I am exactly where I need to be. Thank you for everything you gave me to get me to this place.

Along with gratitude, there are seven practices and routines that keep me grounded and allow me to get through the days and ongoing scans, with a bit of calm and a modicum of sanity. These are things that nourish my soul and help me find balance. They help me to pay attention to mind, body and the creative spirit. These are seven healing commentaries and my priorities. Consistency in practicing them is the key. These practices have become habit, now that I have gone well beyond the 21-day minimum understood to be necessary to create a habit. These healing habits have in themselves become a daily meditation. Disclaimer: Everyone has a different experience and what is helpful to me may or may not be helpful for you. It's best to try things out and see what works for you. These, next to the power of cultivating gratitude, are tips on what works for me for staying calm on a path of peace while living with two brain tumors.

- Mindfulness
- Writing to Discover
- Connecting with My Tribes
- Moving My Body
- Prayer
- Treating Myself
- Dark Humor

*"Knowledge teaches you what to do,
but practice tells you how to do it."*
– Dr. Abraham Low

*"As we express our gratitude, we must never forget
that the highest appreciation is not to utter words
but to live by them. "*
– John F. Kennedy

CHAPTER 15: HEALING COMMENTARY #1:
MINDFULNESS

When I was hired to teach a mindfulness curriculum for an online mental health company, I wanted to help other people. I learned about it the easy way. I read all kinds of books about the practice and its benefits. I enjoyed the experience of teaching others about mindfulness to help them ease their pain. I was familiar with the phrase we teach what we need to learn, but I wouldn't begin my own practice until five or so years later.

I began to practice because I was scared. I had been blindsided by a brain tumor diagnosis after living a privileged, carefree, easy life up until that moment in time. Living with brain tumors is like dropping into a master class in applied mindfulness. The trick is to stay present and not allow myself to get overwhelmed by thoughts about the past trauma of the diagnosis or worry about future trauma of new treatment. Easier said than done.

When I was first released from the hospital, people would check in often to ask how I was doing. I always had the same answer. "Fine, as long as I stay grounded in this present moment."

At the time, I didn't realize or value how much practice that would take. Now I understand. It is not unlike addiction recovery practices, encapsulated by the slogan, "Just for today." "I can refrain from (fill in the blank, drinking, drugging), just for today." I am adjusting the timeframe from a day down to a moment. Just for this moment, I can be aware of the present. It is like sobriety from worry, rather than alcohol or drugs, but it works the same way.

And, like recovery, I am now enrolled in a lifetime program. Scans will likely move out from every four months to every six and then, perhaps every year or even every two or five years. But they will go on for the rest of my life. Unless I choose a different protocol because I always have choices. When my phone chimes with reminders for scan appointments, it gives me three choices: text 1 to confirm, text 2 to reschedule or text 3 to cancel.

I could stop monitoring. Someday I may hit my wall of psychological fatigue and decide to step off the conveyer belt. Right now, I am grateful for access to this world-class testing, so I may as well practice appreciating that privilege, in this present moment awareness.

A mindfulness practice is every hour and every minute of every day. It's being alert to the truth of what is happening in the moment. It is being aware of my internal response to what is happening. I am hearing my spiritual teacher Sylvia Boorstein talking about this very thing as Paisley and I travel happily along on our morning walkie. Sylvia's lessons are streaming through my ears. I am listening to her calming voice. She is narrating her audiobook, *The Courage to Be Happy* and I am certain I am understanding the lessons.

Yes, I am awake. Grateful to be able to walk again. Grateful to get pulled by my strong and beautiful dog without losing my balance. I have a calm mind. Just as I am basking in my new awareness, I notice Paisley has taken this opportunity of my enlightened but distracted joy to find her own.

She has an impressive memory and has returned to the spot called Coyote Rock. It is a large flat rock that sits on the edge of the bridge by the side of the creek. It's a favorite wildlife pooping spot and today there is a large load of fresh scat, multiple piles cover the surface of the rock. It is an interesting collection of berry and fur-filled dung in all its glorious varieties.

"No, Paisley! Damn it!"

I yank her leash and drag her along the ground, away from the collection of coyote leftovers. In this moment, I am angrier at myself than her for forgetting about the pile of poop which has been there for a few days. It was beckoning Paisley as Sylvia was teaching me how to become more mindful.

In a matter of minutes, my inner response to this most unpleasant experience changes from anger and disgust to one of amusement. I burst out laughing and appreciate Paisley's sheer delight in this revolting doggie behavior. I hear Sylvia's calm voice talking in my ear.

Paisley joyfully rolls on her back, belly raised to the sky. It's as if she can't get enough of the seed and berry textured poop which is discoloring her white fur and smearing her red snood brown. She reluctantly wears a cute little red riding hood snood headgear to protect her ears from nasty, burrowing foxtails. She doesn't consider this stinky scat nasty. She is just enjoying her moment, in the roll.

I hear the voice of Sylvia, my favorite mindfulness teacher, float through my mind in her calm Jewish grandmotherly voice. "Remember, be grateful and be happy."

I am glad we have running hot water, a bath tub and baby shampoo waiting for us at home. I am grateful Paisley is used to the bathtub drill, resigned to the consequence as a fair payment for this stinky fun and indulgent roll. She will step over the edge of the tub and get right in without an argument. I will wash away her sins. Imperfect practice. When I was able to laugh, I achieved that feeling of detachment I used to crave so badly, if only for a moment or two.

As I worked out my gratitude and mindfulness practice, there were times when I used to set boundaries and time limits on conscious worrying. I would choose ten minutes, once or twice a day, where the worry was allowed. Sometimes during those worry allowed minutes I would ask myself a question,

"In this very moment, other than your thoughts about past or future, what exactly is the problem?"

The answer was always nothing. The problem was the sound of my thoughts about the future and imagining the thud of the next scan shoe dropping. I am always waiting for the other shoe to drop. I am reminded of the words my mother signed off every conversation we had from the time I got my driver's license at age sixteen, moved into my own place at age twenty until the day she died when I was fifty-six years old. "Check your tires, lock your doors." This was her code for "I love you, stay safe." What I heard is, "It's a dangerous world out there." Today I remind myself; that shoe already dropped. I got two brain tumors. And I am not only surviving, but thriving.

Paisley is a great mindfulness reminder teacher. Her mind is not full like mine. She carries on walking and sniffing, easily pleased with simple things. I must follow, since I am on the other end of the leash. I keep walking. The story I am often telling myself is past or future, not the truth of this moment. When I remember to follow her lead, my mind gets hijacked less often.

The truth of this moment is I am able to walk without wobbling. The truth of this moment, my jeans are dry. Urine is not running down my leg. There are only two things running in this moment, the clear bubbling creek water over smooth and jagged river rocks. And me, trying to keep up with Paisley on her enthusiastic lizard, bug, leaf chasing and poop rolling mission. Paisley the dog teaches me things that I couldn't learn on my own, either from books or in a classroom.

Bernie's voice floats in and I hear him say, "You're better, you couldn't walk when I first met you." In that moment, I remember I am better. I take the next steady step and try to be present. And the next step. And the one after that, higher onto the first railroad tie step and then climbing up to the next one. The truth of this moment isn't complicated. I am balanced, not wobbly. I am dry, not wet, except for the bead of sweat dripping down my back as the hot sun beats down. Thinking is clear, not wacky (or maybe just a little, but in a good way.) I can stop the mind stories of prognoses, diagnoses and scans. It isn't that complicated.

It is as simple as bringing the once wacky mind that couldn't remember what day or year it was into this present moment. Thank you. It is just noticing rather than judging the stories running through my head, in this moment:

- The next scan is two weeks out, time to start worrying.

- The Covid virus numbers are still looking bad, a hospital is the last place I want to be.
- We have been so conscientious with our social isolation and self-imposed staying at home practice. Now I have to enter a hospital and risk all kinds of exposure.

In reality, this present moment is where I am alive. Walking with ease, next to a clear and flowing natural spring creek. I am able to keep my balance even while being pulled by this strong, beautiful, loving dog who looks like a fashionista, even if her snood is now covered in coyote poop. This is Wabi-Sabi. Imperfect perfection.

I stop listening to my audiobook and turn to some happy music to take us back home. The song *Waiting on a Sunny Day* by Bruce Springsteen and the E Street Band pops up. It's the song I played over and over and over before heading into brain surgery. As a musician, Cameron must have been so sick of hearing the bouncy melody and deliberately simple chorus. Knowing it made me feel better, he good-naturedly put up with it. Now I make an effort to only play it and sing along when he isn't in hearing distance. It still makes me happy.

Apparently, I was playing it at the time I was being rolled on a gurney to the operating theater and held up an index fingered "wait-a-second, the song's almost over" gesture to the hospital attendant. I don't remember this, but it has been confirmed by at least two onlookers. Embarrassing.

The sunny day is today. I am alert and present, cognitive faculties intact. The big western sky is a screensaver blue. Thank you. I am not and don't wish to be anyplace else. I am not inside a loud and clanging MRI tube or a hospital with an invisible lurking virus. I am in a place of mindfulness. On a high desert walk. In nature, a place of beauty. A place of happiness, resting in awareness of the present moment.

It doesn't mean I don't have thoughts about Pinena and wonder what she is up to. And it doesn't mean I am pleased about how much she is on my mind. But I am awake and telling the truth about this moment. I am doing the best I can to have what Sylvia calls a wise response to this moment. I love her teachings. She speaks my two favorite languages perfectly. She is bilingual in Jewish and

Buddhist. I hear her voice and I am instantly reminded to be grateful and happy.

I try to emulate Sylvia and inform my life by a gratitude practice. When I am able to do this, I realize it is possible to have health anxieties, scanxiety, and also be grateful, even when the scanxiety sometimes is stronger than the gratitude. It is an imperfect practice, which is why, I guess, they call it practice.

I also hear Dr. Devi Twillresolve's voice in my head, telling me his message, simply through his name. In Buddhist practice, Sylvia says a simple phrase can steer the mind in the direction of insight. Reminder phrases presented by my neurodocs who are also my spiritual teachers set me in the direction of a mind in gratitude and a place of refuge.

It is possible to learn and practice new mind habits, get relief and discover peace of an awakened mind, inside the truth of having a brain tumor and the possibility of needing more than a watch and wait treatment protocol in the future. Life is inevitably challenged with uncertainty, sadness or worry. Like Pinena says, "it can change on a dime." I am more aware now of how fragile day-to-day life can be and how it can be taken away, at any moment. I have a better understanding of the gravity of the emotional impact of this adventure, even though my Parkinson's and dementia-like physical symptoms were miraculously reversed.

Losing my ability to think clearly and control my body functions were potent moments for waking up. What I took for granted and depended on as continuing from day-to-day was illusory. I get that now. It's like one of my fellow brainpeeps said after his transition from his hard-core party frat boy life to new awareness of a brain tumor survivor, "Before the diagnosis, no day was a gift."

CHAPTER 16: HEALING COMMENTARY #2:
WRITING TO DISCOVER

"When you are writing you're trying to find out something which you don't know. The whole language of writing for me is finding out what you don't know, what you don't want to find out. But something forces you anyway."
– James Baldwin

"Memoir is the single greatest portal to self-discovery."
- Marion Roach Smith, *The Memoir Project*

When I was due for my last scan of my first brain recovery year, it was also time to decide if I was going to sign up for the next group session with a writers' community I found through *The Literate Lizard,* my local independent bookstore. During the pandemic, the sessions moved from inside the bookstore to Zoom and we were meeting on Sunday mornings.

The writing teacher called to see if I would be joining the group again. I told him I wanted to hold off until I got my latest scan results before committing to the next six weeks with the community. I swore I wasn't going to live scan to scan anymore, but maybe I should stop swearing. He didn't think that was such a good idea. He reminded me that the book was writing me, not the other way around, and to be open to what arises. He wished me well on the scans, with a local bard-like way and a *Merry Wives of Windsor*-like quote, "As good luck would have it."

I understand at a deeper level now how outcomes, in my case the surgical or scan type, are always influenced by luck, fate and chance. So far, I have been ridiculously lucky. The next day, I told the teacher I would be signing up for the next six-week group. I decided to stop putting life on hold for scan results and hoped my luck would hold out.

This group knew how to keep my spirits up and helped me clarify my purpose in writing. One time, a lovely young Muslim woman member with an interest in writing about conversations with mystics asked a question after I shared a piece of my work:

"So, you are writing a spiritual memoir?"

"What's a spiritual memoir?"

"It seems like the tradition you are working in. It is when you write about your personal experience to find a sacred dimension of that experience."

"Oh, then, yes, I am writing a spiritual memoir. Who knew? I've heard my neurosurgeon describe his job as working with sacred material. I thank him and G-d every single day for my miraculous awakening and cure. So, yeah, I suppose I am writing in that genre."

Writing is a tangible thing I do to manage scanxiety. It's a distraction and a creative act that helps dial it down. I first started writing because I was worried the story might slip away with my cognitive decline. I didn't know the blunt force surgical trauma performed by Dr. Kintsugi would release the water on the brain and give me back my cognition. It was a miraculous reversal. Grateful, I continued to write. I wrote as a form of traveling through the process and the reflective writing has in itself become a means to spiritual growth.

When I first showed up for a half day memoir writing workshop at *The Literate Lizard*, we were asked to introduce ourselves and share a bit about what brought us there. I half joked that I could not afford a real therapist on my modest state retirement income, so I decided to use my daily journals and write my way through my brain tumor trauma, in a therapeutic and healing way. I did this to understand what had happened to me.

I didn't realize it yet, but would soon discover that my tumor Pinena would become my muse. She inspires me to write. There are times when I wish my muse would shrivel up and sometimes, I even wish for her to die. But not until I finish the memoir. Writing with Pinena has brought a lot of joy and powerful insights. The practice and the process has been a transformative healing. I am grateful for the unexpected gift of finding my writer's voice. Thank you, Pinena. And thanks to you too, Pollyanna, for the reminder to say so.

After waking up from brain surgery, I started to journal my experience and chronicle the story, almost right away. The journals became tidal waves of emotional expression. I had to get it all out and privately expressed whatever emotions came into my awareness. The writing ranged from terror and fears about the unknowns to finding a laugh over silly brain tumor humor. I never dreamed my journals would be seen by anyone else, except Cameron. I would sometimes read the journals to him and he helped fill in some gaps in memory. This is his story too; the brain adventure is ours to share.

Then I started to email a series of anecdotes chronicling the adventure to family and friends as a way of staying connected and keeping people informed about my healing. The emails served as an outlet and also became a built-in support group. A prescient prediction by my Aunt Judy came true. The journal entry emails would eventually become the notes for a full-length memoir.

According to Elizabeth Andrew Jarrett in her book *Living Revision, a Writer's Craft as Spiritual Practice*, "the best writing emerges when the stakes are high – when the author writes what is most pressing and heartfelt – because the discovery is correspondingly high." Writing has become a big part of my spiritual practice and can take scanxiety down in a just a few written pages or chapters.

Books and Cuppas

To be a writer, it's important to be a reader. I have always been a bookworm, but now I focused mainly on memoir. And a lot of strong English tea because, as Ivy, my ex's

English Mum used to say, "Where there's tea, there's hope."

Mostly I read other people's brain tumor memoirs. I lost count of how many I read before saying "enough." It was time to write my own story. I poured a cuppa and got ready to write. Then I saw a post on Facebook for yet another brain tumor story. This one was being offered for free for a limited time on Kindle. It was the author's gift to the community during our extended isolation period in the pandemic. I couldn't resist.

It was inspiring, but also a very sad and traumatic story. It was a tale about love and illness and the deadliest kind of brain tumor, the glioblastoma, known as "the terminator or the big bad wolf." The average survival rate with this tumor is only six to eighteen months. The story was filled with lots of detail about post-surgical complications and long-lasting deficits. After finishing the book, I temporarily lost the will to write my story.

I felt like a fraud. An imposter. What is it about unwarranted Jewish guilt? My story felt like brain tumor light. Compared to many of my fellow survivors, I got off so easy. So far, my brain surgery was wildly successful and my tumors have brought me nothing but blessings. The top blessings being the discovery of profound gratitude and finding my voice as a writer.

I gave it a day or two of rest. Then I made a decision to write again. It was therapeutic. I decided to stop comparing myself to other people's stories. I thought about Teddy Roosevelt's famous assertion that "comparison is the thief of joy." I made a decision to only compare myself to who I am now vs. who I was before Bernie opened up my head, pushed his way through my third ventricle and miraculously fixed me. Comparison thinking is deadly for my gratitude. I started to write again, grateful for writing's healing powers.

CHAPTER 17: HEALING COMMENTARY #3:
FINDING MY TRIBES

Tribe members are people who accept us as we are and accompany us on the journey. Among our tribes, we are free to be our imperfect selves. Some of our tribes are there from the beginning and stay a part of us for life. Others we find when we need them. They fulfill one of our basic needs for community. Some for a reason, some for a season and some for life.

From the Buddha to the Baal Shem Tov

I enjoyed exploring my Jewish roots and Buddhist practices as I searched for ways to stay calm while living with brain tumors. I had already read many books on Buddhism and mindfulness in retirement (see chapter on Before the BS).

One Buddhist concept that was confusing is the notion of attachment. Buddhist scholars say detachment is the way to achieve equanimity. Ironically, I was focusing my energy and becoming very attached to detachment. I wanted it badly.

In my confusion, I needed something different. I turned to my Jewish roots.

I signed up for a spiritual book study with the local Chabad rabbi. Chabad is an Orthodox Jewish Hasidic movement, philosophy and organization. Even though I am far more secular than religious, I have always felt warmly welcomed and at home in the Chabad community. In my experience, there is a natural joyful energy surrounding the Hasidic rabbis and their wives I find attractive. It's very different from the religious Judaism I was brought up with, and it is comforting in an inherited and familial way.

The book study class was on *The Tanya*, an early work of Hasidic mystical psychology that can supposedly be used as a guide for daily spiritual Jewish life. I arrived at the class location given to me by the Rabbi, a private home of one of the participants. I knew this was the location because there was a white compact car in the driveway with a four-foot metal menorah attached to the roof. It was Hanukah time. Oy vey.

We sat around the kitchen table which belonged to a beautiful young hipster type woman with long black hair that flowed down her back. Hebrew alphabet letters were tattooed on her knuckles and neck in black ink. She fascinated me but I tried not to stare. She was talkative and seemed to know a lot about Jewish mysticism, the Kabbalah and Tarot. The girl with the Hebrew tattoos. A few weeks after the class I called her to inquire about a tarot reading before one of my scans in a rather desperate move to know my future. She didn't call me back. I don't think the tarot works as fortune telling. Just as well.

I mostly listened as I sat in the class. Everything was new to me. I wanted to observe before engaging. Near the end of the class, the Rabbi turned to me and asked, "What do you know about the Rebbe?"

I wasn't sure what he meant. Was he asking about the author of *The Tanya* book, Rebbe Shneur Zalman? Or did he mean the founder of Hasidism, the Baal Shem Tov?

"Not a lot. I know the Baal Shem Tov was a Jewish mystic and healer and considered the founder of Hasidic Judaism. He brought mysticism from the rabbis and scholars down to everyday people and my ancestors come from the place he was from."

"Do you read Hebrew?"

"Yes, I can read Hebrew language, but don't really understand what I am reading."

I nervously babbled on.

"I am here today to see if studying *The Tanya* might help me cope with my new health anxiety and find inner peace. I am searching for a way to live calmly in my new normal life with the uncertainties of two brain tumors."

Before signing up for the class, I told the Rabbi I was looking for ways to help me cope with my health anxieties in a spiritual way and was wondering if studying *The Tanya* could help with that. He said he couldn't answer that question because he didn't know me very well. He encouraged me to try the class and said *The Tanya* could be a vessel or a container for my learning and spiritual development.

As the class was ending, my head was spinning and I was looking forward to getting back in my car and processing the whole experience. Surprisingly, the rabbi then posed my question to the others.

"She is looking for spiritual direction and wondering if *The Tanya* might be the way."

An elderly man from the class volunteered an answer. "In a nutshell, the answer is unequivocally yes." He gushed about the book as an amalgamation of Jewish wisdom, bringing the Zohar, the chief text of the Kabbalah, the Talmud, the Torah and other mystical teachings together.

He went on enthusiastically about how lucky we were to have this learned mystic, the rabbi, as a teacher in our small town.

In the end, I didn't stick with the class because I felt it was too religious for me. I believe in G-d, but I am more of a cultural and secular Jew. Jewish by birth, I connect to my heritage through the familiar songs of prayers, celebrations of Jewish holidays, music, literature and food. I don't keep Kosher. When I joked with the Rabbi that I was basically a twice-a-year Jew, going to shul on Rosh Hashanah and Yom Kippur. The Rabbi said, "Every Jew is a Jew all year round."

I have been taught that the purpose of Jewish culture is to reduce suffering in the world. It feels shallow to admit this, but as a cultural Jew, I mostly love the food, the music and the melodies of prayer. I like Jewish humor and enjoy occasionally dropping a Yiddish word into conversation. By attending the Talmud and Tanya book study classes, I was hoping to develop a deeper purpose, beyond the cultural loves, but I didn't stick with it. I didn't feel like it was taking me to that deeper place of Tikkun Olam, the idea that Jews bear responsibility not only for their own moral, spiritual and material welfare, but also the welfare of society at large. I wanted to connect to Judaism, but couldn't quite figure out how.

Writing the first draft of this memoir was a focus on personal healing and spiritual welfare. I repeatedly thought about my own brain and health. As I moved into the revision process, I thought more about other people's brains and health, including my mother's shrinking brain and neurological disease. This insight helped me to focus my revision more on the benefit I gained by cultivating gratitude and practicing the seven healing practices. My hope is that sharing what works for me might in some small way reduce suffering and touch others in the brain tumor and chronic illness community. To quote the founder of the *Gray Matters Foundation*, a twenty-year survivor, the underlying motto of our support groups is, "you need hope and support, you give hope and support."

I stay in touch with the rabbi. I exchange emails with his sweet and lovely wife from time to time. She has read pieces of my memoir, mostly the parts about Pinena, and is very encouraging about my writing. When she checks in, she always says,

"Please, G-d, I hope Pinena is behaving herself?"

I love the joyful energy of Chabad and enjoy celebrating Jewish holidays with them.

Cameron and I and my neighbors especially enjoyed the order of delicious prune, poppy and jelly Hamantaschen we received during the Purim holiday this year. The rabbi's wife had packages shipped from a Jewish bakery in Brooklyn, New York. They were the real deal of Jewish comfort food. The Chabad folks are down to earth and always keep it real, even though they live in an otherworldly mystical place. I find that combination fascinating.

We enjoy the celebrations they organize every Hannukah under the holiday lights and sparkly decorations at Tlaquepaque, an upscale collection of galleries, shops and restaurants in Sedona. The rabbi lights the candles on a portable giant outdoor menorah, hires a Klezmer band for entertainment and serves home-made latkes, jelly donuts, hot chocolate and apple cider. It's the highlight of our holiday season.

The Brain Peep Fellowship

Before my brain surgery, I wasn't active on social media. I didn't even have a Facebook account. I had some lingering fears around Cameron's many exes reading about our happiness, so I stayed out of that world.

After brain surgery, I joined several brain tumor online support groups and found enormous connection, hope and a shared experience with people I will likely never meet in person. Some I don't even know their real names, only their pseudonyms or avatars.

I obviously would not have chosen to belong to this group of friends who I lovingly refer to as my Brainpeeps. But do I ever appreciate them being there. It is a comforting sense of solidarity with people who walk my walk and talk my talk. How odd that we can converse at such intimate levels and never even meet in person.

We speak a kind of shorthand with each other, without having to draw out long explanations. Brainpeeps know the difference between feeling tired and neuro-fatigue. In our house, we call it Fat-A-Gyoo. I am used to living with autoimmune disease fatigue, but this is Ankylosing Spondylitis fatigue times ten. Brainpeeps understand it is not a tiredness that can be cured by a triple shot expresso at Starbucks or a good night's sleep. Tired from overthinking everything and never knowing what is coming next. Tired from wondering if it is just a headache, a stiff neck or an ankylosing spondylitis flare-up. Tired from the inflammation running rampant through my body. I am profoundly grateful, but no matter how big my gratitude is, I am tired.

Invisible deficits are something we brainpeeps learn to live with and compensate for. Mine are mostly residual visual perception deficits. Sometimes it can feel like I am sitting in the front row of an IMAX theater. Suddenly there will be a flash of light or a surreal bug-eyed giant bug will pop out of nowhere and I'll try to swat it away. Often times I'll reflexively lean-in toward the driver while sitting in the passenger seat of a car, afraid we are too close to passing cars or large trucks parked on the side of the road. I am hyper-vigilant with my self-control about refraining from saying out loud, "watch out!" Open cabinets, drawers, and other pop-outs at eye level are always a worry. These are minor residual visual deficits I gratefully accept.

A few times a month I participate in live online support groups organized by the following groups:

- National Brain Tumor Society
  (https://braintumor.org/)
- The Ivy Brain Tumor Center at Barrow's Neurological Hospital
  (https://www.ivybraintumorcenter.org/)
- Gray Matters, a non-profit Phoenix based organization
  (https://www.graymattersfoundation.org/)
- Every day I find a new email message from the Team Inspire forum, where I read about tips, treatments and stories from members in the American Brain Tumor Association
  (https://www.abta.org/community).

Being a part of these groups made up of brain tumor survivors and caregivers is a humbling, uplifting and sometimes sad experience. Powerful. It is humbling to witness the strength, positive energy and humor in these groups. It fills my heart up.

I belong to a memoir Writing Accountability Group called WAG. It's a diverse group of talented, interesting and creative women whose writing and stories are uplifting and sometimes plain brilliant. We meet in the mornings to quietly work on our memoirs. Once a week, we share our writing as well as resources and tips on the craft. Author Marion Roach was right. The memoir writing project has become the greatest single portal to my self-discovery. Sharing that experience with like-minded people involved in their creative process has been a joy.

CHAPTER 18: HEALING COMMENTARY #4: MOVE YOUR BODY AND QUIET THE MIND

"If all you can do is crawl, start crawling."
— Rumi

As I recovered, I started out doing laps around our community tennis courts on my candy apple red Rollater walker. Eventually, I was able to pick up the leash again. It felt good to get pulled along by Paisley on the high desert trails along the natural spring creek just outside our community. I started to see the trails in a different way, sometimes overwhelmed by the stark natural beauty of the high desert. I named my favorite hike "Gratitude Trail." When I shared this with my neighbors, they erected a pile of rocks at the start of the trailhead, a cairn marker.

I wondered how far we were walking. Then I discovered a built-in pedometer app on my phone that I always carry in my pocket. The app tracks and graphs each step and shows the distance in miles. 10,000 steps per day, I learned, was a noble daily goal. Maybe it's akin to the "apple a day keeping the doctor away" expression. It certainly was worth a try. The pedometer shows up as a bar graph. It starts out with the color red. It gradually turns orange as you walk toward your goal and then turns to a bright lime green as you mark your progress. When you reach the 10,000[th] step, the solid green bar is tall and you are celebrated with a cascading shower of green confetti that rains down the screen for a full ten seconds. I started to obsess on seeing the confetti reward.

10,000 steps amounted to a little more than four miles for someone with my stride. It sounds like a lot, but it wasn't any longer than our regular walkies. Seeing the green bars and confetti started to feel like such an accomplishment. But being the obsessive person that I am, I started to push it and decided to increase the goal to five miles. I split the walks up into two outings, an early morning one before the killer Arizona heat begins and a slightly shorter evening one at sundown.

I go further in the morning because Cameron usually accompanies us on evening walkies and he isn't obsessed like I am.

"Why isn't 10,000 steps and green confetti enough anymore? It's hot out here."

"Because," replies the obsessive me. "I guess I could change Paisley's name to Five Miles. Then I could say I'm out walking Five Miles every day, twice a day."

A few days later I noticed an orange bar on the pedometer. I was shocked to see it, then I remembered getting a late start the day before, and thinking I'd finish up the last 1000 steps after the 2-hour brain tumor support group meeting. By 8 pm, I was knackered and had just enough energy to flop down on the couch after microwaving our delish turkey pot pie "dinner for two." Cameron had presented me with this beautiful all-in-one meal that afternoon, along with a bright bouquet of fresh flowers from Safeway, just because. He is such a romantic.

I had forgotten the last 1,000 steps to green. At first sight the next morning, my horror almost immediately turned to relaxation when I remembered, oh yeah, I'm living wabi-sabi now. There it is. A long row of perfect green bars interrupted by one perfectly imperfect orange spike; a goal unfinished.

After becoming wobbly, losing the ability to walk on my own and then having it miraculously restored, I am grateful I can walk five miles a day. This routine is also part of my spiritual practice and it too has the power to keep me awake, mindful and dial down the scanxiety with every single step.

CHAPTER 19: HEALING COMMENTARY #5: PRAYER

"The more we come alive and awake, the more everything we do becomes prayer.
Eventually even our prayer will become prayer."
– Brother David Steindl-Rast

One of my rabbis tells a story about how she was warned not to use the words *G-d* or *Spiritual* when she was interviewing for rabbinical school. I heeded the same warning as I began to write my story because I worried about offending my mostly atheist family and friends. But this is my story, so I must tell what is true for me.

When I was a little girl, my childhood best friend and I used to sing Jewish prayers, loud, off-key and with gusto, while sitting on the outdoor breezeway that separated our working-class apartment buildings. I lost that joy and enthusiasm when my mother remarried and we moved to the ritzier suburbs where the religious experiences became more about materialism and status.

Now I am rediscovering Jewish prayers learned in my

childhood. I have always loved the melody of the prayers and the beautiful lettering of the Hebrew language. Today they take on new meaning. I read or say three prayers in the morning (see below) to set my intention and cultivate gratitude throughout the day. The prayers are scotch-taped to my bathroom mirror and are usually the first things I see in the morning. Taped alongside them is an inspirational quote by the Baal Shem Tov, posted there when I was still wobbly.

Let me fall if I must. The one I will become will catch me.

To the left of the quote and prayers, dangling from a black satin cord attached to the light fixture is a healing pewter prayer wheel pendant with three spinning beads for meditating. The Hebrew text is taken from the *Mi Shebeirakh* prayer for healing, the words heal, restore, strengthen and enliven revolve around the phrase "healing of the body, healing of the soul." The prayer wheel talisman, designed by artist Emily Rosenfeld, is meant to help focus the power of faith and love towards healing.

Modeh Ani: ancient Jewish prayer of gratitude said upon wakening. The Orthodox Jewish tradition believes the soul leaves us at night and we are blessed if it is returned to us, refreshed, in the morning. I open my eyes, and before getting out of bed, my mind focuses. I realize I'm alive and the breath of life is compassionately returned. My lips begin to move and I say thank you, with mindfulness. I have an opportunity to make peace between my body and soul for another day and shine my light where I can.

Modeh Ani. L'fanecha. Melech Chai v'Kayam. She-he-che-zarta Bee. Nishmati. B'chemla. Raba Emunatecha.

Benching Ha Gomel: a beautiful Jewish tradition of expressing gratitude and relief. It is a blessing of thanks for surviving something perilous (brain surgery), a situation of grave danger (obstructive hydrocephalus) and recovery from a serious illness.

Baruch Atah Adonai, Eloheinu Melech ha-olam, ha-gomel l'chayavim tovim she-g'malani kol tov.

Shehecheyanu: a blessing that is recorded in the Talmud and has been recited by our tribe for over 1500 years. It encourages Jews to offer thanks for new and unusual experiences and for the time when we realize the miracle of the present moment.

Baruch Atah Adonai, Eloheinu Melech haolam, shehechehyanu, v'key'manu, v'higiyanu laz'man hazeh.

CHAPTER 20: HEALING COMMENTARY #6: TREAT YOURSELF

Treats look different in a pandemic. Hopefully, I will be able to get back to the traditional treats one day. Before Covid, I would splurge on a pre-MRI good luck holistic pedicure. My psychic pedicurist believes it is possible to disappear tumors through manifesting beliefs. I don't believe that, but I do love choosing good luck colors from her sample wheel of painted nails, just before going in for the next MRI.

She always asks if I want extra sparkles. I do, but I turn them down because I worry about the metallic flecks setting off the magnets in the scanner machine. I settle for a beautiful color and relaxing foot treatment. The Sedona experience includes a tuning fork healing. The pedicurist strikes the two-pronged fork against her palm and then places the vibrating U-shaped bar over my bunions. This acoustic resonator supposedly raises my vibration and brings harmony to my body on an intracellular level.

Up until the pandemic, our trips to the Mayo were like mini vacations. We had sleepovers with our bestie Greg and went out to Chompie's Jewish Delicatessen with my family for comfort food of white fish salad and toasted bagels with scallion cream cheese. We followed up with a Rugalach treat or black and white cookies from their bakery. We visited bookstores and ZIA Record Exchange; a vintage music store that feels like a time travel return to the 1970s.

Another one of our ritual stops took us further back in time, to the 1950s, inside See's Candies Shop. I loved buying boxes of gratitude gift chocolates for Drs. Bendok and Porter. The shop is clean and spotless with an almost medically sterile feel, except for the aroma of freshly made chocolates that waft through as soon as you open the door. The staff, stout older women, wear starched white uniforms and little white caps reminiscent of nurse uniforms from a different era. They circulate throughout the store, wearing warm inviting smiles and offering up trays of freshly-made irresistible gooey and nutty caramel and chocolate concoctions. The displays are seasonal and I usually pick out the classic boxes that come gift-wrapped with shiny gold wrapping and big, sparkly festive bows for my neurodocs/spiritual teachers.

I can't wait for the day we can get back to all of these traditional treat rituals. In the meantime, I treat myself by buying more books online and brain tumor awareness face masks and t-shirts.

CHAPTER 21: HEALING COMMENTARY #7: (DARK) HUMOR WITH THE TUMOR AND THE BLESSING OF LAUGHTER

Warning to the reader: This section contains profanity. If you think you may find it offensive, please just skip to the next chapter. I don't think it is gratuitous profanity, but I'm from New Jersey.

Be who you are and say what you feel, because those who mind don't matter and those who matter don't mind.
– Dr. Seuss

Everyone knows laughter and humor is the best medicine and has the power to heal. I read some place that when we laugh, we are giving ourselves over to the immediacy of the present moment because laughter involves the whole body, emotions and soul all at once.

One of my favorite games to play is "Is my headache from dehydration, Ankylosing spondylitis, caffeine withdrawal, lack of proper nutrition, my ponytail, stress, lack of sleep, not wearing my glasses or brain tumor?"

Pinena and Pollyanna are in good company, as many in the community name our tumors. Most have male names.

Timmy is a common one. Beotch is popular. People will post funny things, like, "Surgery scheduled for two weeks. Derek you're outta here." Or "Good riddance to my mate Gary. Cheers, motherf%u&cker!" One I like a lot is a simple, "Bye, Felicia." I remember laughing out loud when reading about one particularly nasty tumor residing in a lady's head that she named Trump. She explained, even though he invaded her head just like he did the rest of the world, at least she was getting the opportunity soon to cut him out.

Tumor humor is my new genre. I laugh over dark jokes, memes, videos and writing that I don't even want to admit makes me laugh. A favorite coffee mug turned pen and pencil holder is one I custom-designed online. It's an image of a brain, with the text "Pinena...50% Namaste and 50% FOH." I am glad I no longer feel like I need to change or cover up my cynical sense of irony. It is perfectly acceptable now that I am a brain tumor survivor.

According to the Urban Dictionary, FOH stands for "Fu&% outta here" and is mostly used as a phrase when someone is mad over some bulls*it. Like getting a brain tumor. If you happen to be from Jersey, like me, you probably already knew the meaning.

I originally found this sentiment embodied in a funny online meme. It was an image of a Buddhist monk. His head was shaved and he wore a flowing ankle length saffron robe. He was jaywalking between parked cars and dodging traffic on a congested urban street. With his middle finger, he was flipping off the moving cars honking at him. The text read: *"Looks like somebody overslept and missed their morning loving-kindness meditation today."*

I broke up laughing again when I found an internet GIF of Pauly Walnuts, mobster character of Sopranos fame, mouthing the FOH with a mildly rude hand gesture under his chin. Sitting next to him, side-by-side, was the image of Theresa of *The Real Housewives of New Jersey* fame. She wore heavy face and eye make-up, big hair and prison garb. Her hands were folded in prayer pose and she mouthed the word Namaste. Yup, sums it up for me and Pinena, 50% FOH, 50% Namaste.

My cousin recently gave me a book recommendation she thought I would enjoy. She said David Sedaris's essays in his book *Calypso* were darker than his earlier work and contained bits on tumor humor. She was right, I was laughing out loud in a few parts.

The Brain Tumor Card (BTC)
aka The Golden Pass

The brain tumor card is like our National Parks Lifetime Golden Passport. It works in powerful ways. It is like the way a new low-puff down jacket keeps you safe and warm in winter. You put on the down jacket, and it ends all argument. You know you're going to be cozy and comfortable in the cold. Present the BTC and you are off the hook, safe and comfortable.

Have a social engagement you don't feel like doing? Drop the card, you're automatically free. Forgot the names of your new neighbors whom you just met the other day? Pull the card and you're instantly excused. Want to have a lovely lie-in and stay in a warm bed until noon with books and cuppas or an afternoon nap on the couch, use the card. It's a free pass.

The BTC concept came up as a topic at a recent support group meeting. I am the only member, as far as I know, on a WaWa plan and without a cancer diagnosis. I am told the BTC with accompanying cancer diagnosis gets a super-charged power, especially when you are wishing to instill a bit of extra-strength guilt. As I droned on a bit about how difficult it was to stay calm while WaWa'ing, I was one-upped in a good-natured and humorous way by a 20-year survivor who is forever in WaWa Land for a cancer disease recurrence. Touché!

There is a risk of overusing the card and I have stepped over that line a time or two or three. I am sure there have been times where I am that annoying friend or relative with the brain tumor, but my peeps are too kind and generous to say so. It's a fine line to walk. I thank G-d and I thank Bernie that I can walk a line, even if I overstep the boundaries from time to time.

Certain social events don't require the BTC because it's an event you always want to attend. Virtually everyone in the community celebrates brainaversaries. Unfortunately, my one-year milestone celebration was canceled this year due to Covid-19. It was supposed to be held at our favorite funky Bar-B-Que joint, once featured in Diners, Drive-ins and Dives. We discovered and fell in love with this place during our Emerald City stay. I will never forget my May

3, 2019, day of goodness, gratitude and infamy. Next year, at The Thumb, G-d willing.

Brainpeeps can get very creative with brain tumor cycle celebrations. One pre-op "coming out" party shared on one of my fellow survivor pages featured home-made cupcakes topped with swirly icing formed into the shape of a brain and soft marshmallow centers to pop out, just like a tumor removal. This is one social event I'd love to get an invitation to and a party I'd show up for too.

Part IV

Aging Gratefully in the Mystery

CHAPTER 22: RETURN TRIPS TO SCANXIETYLAND

August 2019 – Scanxiety Visit #1

Today's MRI follow-up meeting with Dr. Porter takes place inside the Oncology wing. There are storefront spaces that look like pop up shops, displaying merchandise designed to cover cancer side effects; hats, head coverings, scarves, clothing and wigs. A woman is standing in the lounge area, talking loudly on her cell phone, complaining about not wanting to change to a new chemo drug because of her fear of unknown side effects. She is complaining about the unfairness of it all.

I don't like being in this space, even though there are huge picture windows with beautiful sweeping mountain views of the city. I have fears about tumor growth, cancer and treatment plans other than WaWa, where the only challenge is learning how to stay calm. I don't think I have the fortitude for another brain surgery or any scenario involving the pain and discomfort of radiation or sickness from chemotherapy.

We are led into the consult room by a lovely volunteer, a senior woman heavily made up with her hair swept up in a long blonde complicated up-do. She "treats" us to a bubbly monologue about the history and glory of the Mayo Clinic, all the wonderful new cancer treatments, the construction of new floors in the hospital expansion, the state-of-the-art cancer library on the ground floor and the fabulous cancer resource people whose job it is to guide patients through every step of the process. She asks if we have visited the library or met with the patient guides yet. I shake my head no.

She is hard selling the Mayo experience, and I want to say, "Please stop talking. We're already sold."

Instead I stay silent and let her ramble on. She intimates that she was once on "our side of the couch" and her purpose now is to give back in gratitude. I am waiting for her to draw breath and stop talking long enough for me to tell her that it is unlikely I have cancer, but I never get the chance. She takes my vitals; says I have a slight fever of 99 degrees and asks me if I feel warm. I shake my head no, but think to myself, well, it is 117 degrees outside. She makes notes for my chart, wishes us well and leaves the room.

Dr. Porter enters and immediately says, in her inimitable direct, no-nonsense awesome way,

"Your MRI is stable."

I want to hug her. She always gets right down to business and tells us exactly what we came here to find out. Her eyes crinkled up as she smiled and I felt my own body and mind start to relax. I know I can stay safely on my WaWa plan and continue to grow in my practice and strengthen techniques for staying calm, with Dr. Porter by my side.

Dr. Porter pulls up my scan on her monitor to show us the images. She uses the cursor and points to Pinena, noting no change in size or shape. Pinena seems large when displayed on such a big screen. Dr. Porter makes no mention of Pollyanna.

"What are those large dark things that look like butterfly wings?"

"Those are your ventricles."

I am thinking about the classic butterfly metaphor for personal cycles of transition, transformation and renewal. I am happy. Dr. Porter is pleased too. I am also apprehensive, wondering about Dr. Bendok's perspective. I find my courage to express this fear.

"What if Dr. Bendok wants to go back in for tumor biopsy or removal?"

"Then I will say, Bernie, I am not eager to go back in there."

She tells me exactly what I want to hear. She rocks. We exchange a bit of small talk and commiserate about the heat. She tells us the schools are keeping her kids inside because it is too hot to let them out to play, so they have all kinds of pent up energy. She is human. She is real. She is kind and relatable. She is my advocate and I love her.

November 2019 -Scanxiety Visit #2

"Ain't nothing wrong with that brain." This is something said by readers who have been on the receiving end of my email ramblings of gritty impressions and raw feelings. They are very generous and I appreciate their kindness. Many said I was brave, but I had no choice. It is my neurodocs who are the brave ones. They make the choice to do this work.

My neurodocs and I know there is something wrong with my brain. I am using my brain to understand what is wrong with my brain. Truly understanding the human brain is impossible. According to my friend Susanne's late brilliant father, a radiologist with a master's degree in physics, this is because the brain can't understand itself. To understand something, you have to be in some sense outside of it.

I may not be able to understand it, but I know the technique of creative writing is helping my brain in the recovery process. It helps keep me focused and grateful for my tumor "gifts."

Although I haven't yet worked up the nerve to share the naming of my tumors with my neurodocs, I decided to share a short piece of my writing with them on this Scanxiety trip to the clinic.

> "Once upon a time in Alice's Wonderland, Humpty Dumpty tells Alice that slithy means lithe and slimy. And mimsy is flimsy and miserable. Two words, packed together, like two halves of a traveling suitcase, a portmanteau. My new portmanteau is Scanxiety. It is the traveling suitcase on my Through the Looking Glass adventure.

Once upon another time, a brilliant scientist named Schrodinger came up with the now famous thought experiment called Schrodinger's Cat. In his experiment, a cat inside a box can be dead and alive. In my world, a tumor inside my brain can be dead and alive, growing or shrinking. Schrodinger says more than one thing can be true at the same time. It has something to do with quantum mechanics and the only way to tell what is true is to go inside the box and have a look.

It is the observation that determines the outcome and we can't know what is happening until we take a look inside. My box is the dreaded MRI tube, my brain tumor is the cat and my brilliant neurodocs are the ones who will take a look inside. The doctors are treating the body and it's my job to figure out how to treat my mind and soul.

Scanxiety is my companion in this new world. Did the tumor grow? Did it shrink? Did it stay the same? Could it once again be what they call "stable," which is my favorite word in the English language and the luckiest word of the day?

Scanxiety is like a spiritual practice. It's like cultivating the "don't-know mind," in the spirit of Zen. It's uncertainty. It's hope. Mostly, it's learning how to be okay with that, in the curiouser and curiouser WaWa world. Watch and Wait. And trust."

Dr. Porter thanks me for the chocolates and tells me my writing is a beautiful gift. "And I will let you in on a little secret. We get scanxiety too."

When I gave Bernie his gifts, he thanked me and asked questions about the writing. He was curious about the process. "Do I write in longhand? Do I type it up?"

I told him it is like a private blog and he is often featured in the story. Just as my existence has been made richer by the care and compassion of my neurodocs, I hope I can add richness to their lives through creatively expressing my profound gratitude for them.

2020—The Strangest of Times, All the Way 'Round; Breaking Up with Dr. Kintsugi on Another Scanxiety Return Trip

January 31, 2020 Scanxiety Visit #3

A tall, dark, young and handsome Mediterranean looking man with a slight and unrecognizable accent enters the consult room and introduces himself as Dr. Bernie's intern-fellow. He read my file and summarized my case. My scans show stable tumors. He asks permission to do the neuro eval. Today he is the opening act for our rock star. He moves closer and holds out his hands for me to push and pull on them.

"What's the relationship between you two?"

Cameron and I look at him with blank expressions. Cameron speaks first.

"Well, we're not married, but we have been together for thirteen years and we act married..."

I interrupt, "He is my superhero."

"Oh, I wish I could be a superhero." He paused for a moment and said, "Well, I guess I am one, at least for now. I have a two- and four-year-old. I suppose I am their superhero, but I know that won't last too long."

After the touch your nose, touch my hand, walk a straight line towards the door, toe to toe, close your eyes, I stand still and steady as I get a light push. I sit back down on the couch, next to Cameron, and settle in for the film. He pulls up my latest scan and tilts the large desk monitor towards us so we have a better view. It was amazingly detailed with layers and layers of brain, down to the veins in my head. Modern medicine imaging is quite miraculous and it no longer freaks me out to see the inside of my brain on the big screen. Instead, I experience a sense of wonder now.

The way he navigated made it appear like a real-time video, with movement and flow. He pointed out the gap, a small notch in the third ventricle. You could almost see how the cerebral spinal fluid would drain through it. Breathtaking.

In his medical jargon, it's patent. That means it is working as it should. And stable. Dr. Handsome Mediterranean points out Pinena, sitting still, quiet and on good behavior in dead center of my brain. Then he points out Pinena's sister, a skull-based schwannoma, also stable. This is Pollyanna, but she hasn't been named yet.

It took almost a year to come out of my denial about Pollyanna's existence. Like my doctors, I believed her to be too small and insignificant to merit a name. Soon after this meeting though, I will discover her reason for being and give her a proper name, Pollyanna. She will be a constant reminder of my will to cultivate gratitude dream.

We chat about my health and how well I've been doing these past three months, watching and waiting. Medicine is powerful and so is the mind. Bernie did his part with the brain and the body and I am doing my part with the mind and spirit.

I proudly share how I am able to walk my dog four or five miles a day, engage in creative writing about my experience, engage in mindfulness relaxation techniques and practice living a wabi-sabi lifestyle.

We talk about aging, the importance of keeping the brain active and how tumors generally behave. It is becoming clearer to me that I will likely die WITH a brain tumor, not FROM a brain tumor. With the power of these prepositions, I feel lighter and more hopeful than ever.

After the meeting, Cameron and I will share that we both flashed back to the first time I was pushed and pulled in a neuro eval by a different intern during my first exam in pre-surgery days, resulting in a tumbling backward and the ugly-cry on the consult floor. I've come a long way in ten months. The best part of coming through this adventure is being aware and alive, with Cameron steadfast by my side, sharing the memories and the experience, intense and traumatic as they are.

Dr. Handsome Mediterranean leaves to brief Bernie on our interview. Soon there is another knock on the door.

Our rock star enters, in full scrubs, sniffling and apologizing for not shaking hands. He has a cold. I think to myself, *Damn, I would not want to be operated on by a person with a cold, brilliant as this man is. One unexpected sneeze and... whoopsie, there go your memories!*

I know it wouldn't really be like that.

He tells us about another patient he has with a pineal tumor who is not adjusting as well. You can see the pain in his face. Her anatomy, unlike mine, isn't spacious enough for an ETV, so he will be implanting a shunt inside her brain.

I had no idea about this aspect of brain anatomy and am blown away, once again, by how freaking lucky I am on so many different levels, like space being available in the anatomy of my ventricles. First and foremost, it is always luck. And just like it is always a question of luck, the right answer is always gratitude. Thank you, spacious ventricles.

I had no plans to say this to Bernie, but for some reason I suddenly blurt out, "You know that I love you, but I don't want to go back in the theater with you."

Here comes the breakup. I am looking directly at Bernie, so I can't see Cameron, but I know he is cringing and once again hiding his face in his hands. I am just being honest and expressing my feelings. He is a surgeon and I don't want any more brain surgery. I think Bernie understands.

As my beautiful, smart, kind, generous and insightful psychiatrist-cousin Liz will later explain, this is like my toddler rapprochement phase in brain tumor psychological development. Intuitively, I know I need autonomy and I need the security of Bernie's support. Step away, reach back. Move further away, but only with the confidence that comes with the knowledge that my neurodoc caregiver is still there. I know he will be, even as we separate. Damn, my cousin is brilliant and I am so lucky she is in my life. She helps me sort through the beauty and the muck. I only hope I can be there for her one day.

I try to lighten the mood of this breakup meeting by telling Bernie I have a joke for him. "How long does it take to recover from brain surgery?" I wait a few seconds while he thinks about this and then I deliver the punchline. "How long is a piece of string?"

The room is silent.

"That's the joke."

Bernie just looks at me with a bemused half-smile expression. This joke has now flopped in three different venues: Greg's living room, the ritual family meal restaurant table at Chompie's Jewish Delicatessen and now the neurosurgery consult room. I guess it's one of those "you had to be there" jokes that only brain tumor survivors find funny.

Bernie says that I should come back and see him in a year. We can continue to communicate by portal email and he will read my quarterly scans. He asks me to email him as they get scheduled so he can access and review the reports. He tells me Dr. Porter will be following me closely now. I know he is still on my team.

The last line of the story I gave to my neurodocs today was "It doesn't get easier, you get stronger."

Dr. Porter added, "You are right, it doesn't get easier, WE ALL get stronger."

CHAPTER 23: FRIENDS AND FAMILY

The Book-babes

As I was first recovering in the hospital, I somehow managed to find a life-changing memoir eBook on my Kindle. I have no idea how I found it and don't remember downloading it. I only remember being profoundly grateful for being able to read.

This was before I learned from my fellow Brainpeeps that I was supposed to be limiting screen time to help my brain recover. Sitting in front of a computer or phone screen after brain surgery increases inflammation. According to my fellow travelers, staying away from all digital screens for two to three weeks post-op is best for good recovery outcomes. Who knew? It's kind of amazing the things the doctors don't tell you. But I'm glad I didn't know. Otherwise, I wouldn't have experienced the thrill and gratitude to find out I could still read.

The book, *Stir: My Broken Brain and the Meals That Brought Me Home* by Jessica Fechtor is a memoir of a young Jewish woman's recovery from a brain aneurysm. She tells how she used cooking and baking to nourish and strengthen herself back to health after her brain explosion. She weaves delicious recipes into each chapter. I mostly skimmed over them since I don't cook or bake. We could go hungry if not for the microwave oven.

I shared the astonishing news that I could still read with my book club friends, the book-babes from the *No Rules Book Club*. I didn't think it would be a book selection for the group, too gritty, gruesome and raw, but I thought they might enjoy the recipes.

Every single one of the babes, with the exception of myself and one other woman who rarely attends anymore, is a phenomenal cook and baker. I am sure I was the only one to be mystified as to why the grocery store shelves that normally hold flour and yeast were empty at the beginning of the Covid pandemic. Our gatherings are as much about sharing delicious food and wine as book discussions.

To my surprise, *Stir* was selected for our September book. I tried to dissuade the babes from this this choice. It was too raw and too close to the bone for me. But these ladies are pretty powerful. Ruth previewed it on her own and insisted it would be a good group read. I was terrified.

I knew it would be impossible to get through a meeting without emotionally breaking down. I was still pretty fragile. I couldn't very well skip the meeting when it was technically my book suggestion. The only way out, I thought, would be to start writing up my own story so that I could read instead of having to talk, cry or sob. Yes, reading my own journal writing, which I had been doing privately all along, would be the way to go. And a memoir was born.

When the time came for the meeting, the setting was the gorgeous *Seven Canyons Resort* restaurant nestled inside the Coconino National Forest lands. It was a perfect sunny day in a magical place. We were seated in the restaurant's outdoor patio among the grandeur of the naturally sculpted red rocks of Sedona. We settled in with our lunches and I felt completely comfortable among these warm, supportive and nurturing friends. I thought I could read my writing.

Not only are the book-babes kind, smart and funny, they are also over the top creative. Michelle brought book-themed party gifts for all of us, a variety of big wooden spoons with a hand-made poem, a recipe for friendship, printed on a tag and attached to each spoon with a blue satin ribbon. A month earlier, Ruth had created the most amazing compilation of Jessica Fechtor's recipes and put it all together in a booklet format for me. I treasure this treasure. I haven't tried my hand at cooking any of the delicious recipes yet, but there is always hope.

As we sat around our table after lunch, I read my journals aloud and shared a level of vulnerability and intimacy I didn't know was possible before my somewhat rude "awakening." We laughed and cried together. I can't even begin to express the gratitude and love I feel for this special, kind and generous community of friends.

I didn't have literary aspirations before this journey began. I just knew I had to get it all out, everything that was inside of me, processing this powerful and traumatic experience. After our lunch gathering, I started sending out more journal musings to the Book Babes. I worried I was sending them out too often and pictured the beloved babes seeing my notes pop into their in-boxes and thinking, "Not again!"

Last Christmas I sent an email offer out to readers of my writing/therapy notes. The subject line was "Please cancel my subscription to your issues." I had seen this funny line on t-shirt in a holiday catalogue. I tried to express my love and gratitude for their generosity, kindness and patience with the many musings I was sending out as I progressed in my brain recovery. And I wanted to let them off the hook.

I have inundated family and friends over the year with all kinds of musings about my tumors, my surgery and how my life has changed forever. Everyone received these raw and unedited musings with grace and patience.

"I think maybe I will cut back a bit on sending out my musings in 2020."

"You won't, you can't help yourself," said the all-knowing Cameron.

These journals were my therapy. Some of my fellow brain buddies asked me to join as a guest blogger on their public platforms, a more public space where it could potentially help a larger audience. I was flattered and although I admired their ability to put themselves out there with the intimate and the raw, that was beyond my comfort zone of a small group of family and friends.

Truth be told, it will take a lot more courage than I imagined to be brave enough to push the manuscript towards publishing. Control much? I am further down the road and learning to live wabi-sabi, more curious than fearful about seeing how things play out with Pinena and feeling more comfortable with each passing day with sharing in a public space.

Three months after my first public reading of my journal musings, our *No Rules Book Club* group returned to *Seven Canyons*, once again at Ellen's generous invitation. We gathered inside for our holiday celebration of tea, Chinese take-out and book discussion of *The Tea Girl of Hummingbird Lane* by Lisa See. Later, as we toured Ellen's gorgeous and impeccably decorated rustic chic townhouse timeshare, Suzanne leaned over and whispered in my ear,

"Are you writing the book?"

"Absolutely not! That would be like having sex in public!"

The next month Suzanne joined me for an afternoon workshop on memoir writing at *The Lizard*, our local independent bookstore in Sedona. I was surprised to see her there. I was thrilled to know she too was thinking about writing a memoir. She said she was only there to support me. I was overwhelmed and grateful for her friendship. Suzanne has a calming energy about her that always makes me feel a sense of peace and healing in her presence.

Less than a year later, it is the first night of Rosh Hashanah, a time to remember to be grateful, to take stock of the past year and look forward to the year ahead. The first draft of my therapeutic healing manuscript is nearly done. Cameron and I park our RV on the Pinos creek that runs through Suzanne's spectacular sprawling Colorado mountain ranch. Her new friend Pecos and a lovely couple from Sedona are also visiting and staying in the cabin with Suzanne. At sundown, we all gather on the outdoor patio, facing the massive gray back mountain, dip apples into honey and wish each other a sweet, healthy and happy new year.

I whisper a soft Hebrew prayer beneath my breath for the new year, thank G-d and Bernie for my healing and set my *kavanah*, or intention, for the new year. I am better. My intention is to be better next year. The southeastern Colorado ranch, surrounded by the moving water of the creek and tall, 9,000-foot snow-capped mountains is a perfect peaceful setting to set my intentions to gracefully accept the beauty and impermanence of this very imperfect perfect world. And so, the ten days between the Jewish New Year and Yom Kippur begin. I silently pray for gratitude, calm and patience in my WaWa journey. I ask for forgiveness I lack. I forgive and vow to do better.

Suzanne's new friend Pecos tells me he had given her a new name and is calling her CW. He says I should call my graceful friend CW too.

"What does CW stand for?"

"Calming woman."

The Extended Fam

A core group of family supported me emotionally through it all and I am grateful for all the love and support I receive from them. They always gave me what I needed to ease my mind. My brother Michael, sister-in-law Jan and niece Jenn made up Team Arizona. The Team Philly Power crew was a triumphal arch of Aunt Judy, Aunt Debbie and cousin Liz. Team Earnshaw rooted me on too: Lester, Dell, Joanne, Jim and of course, my in-patient honorary neuro-nurses extraordinaire, Carly and Lilly.

I have taken these amazing people for granted at one time in my life. I now have a deep understanding that having them in my life and sharing my adventure are benefits and blessings that I did absolutely nothing to merit or deserve. I want to express my deepest gratitude to all of them.

Three Jersey Girls, One Jersey Boy and a Phoenix Oldie but Goodie Rock

Old and solid friends are the best. You especially appreciate them when you reach my age and realize you are too old to be making any new friends who will become old friends. These are the kinds of friends you can go months or even years without talking and when you reconnect nothing has changed.

Elisa, the "other" Susan, Nancy and, of course, David are my beloved Jersey peeps who have been good and solid friends for more than forty years. They have all been there for me through the whole brain journey. Their friendship is one of life's most precious gifts.

Nancy was a new-age thinker before I'd ever heard the term. She is a retired medical social worker with a huge heart, a ton of wisdom and even more compassion. When I express a bit of frenetic anxiety about not healing quickly enough, she reassures me I am healing in the exact right amount of time. She thinks I may be experiencing post-traumatic stress and tells me she had it quite bad after her cancer treatment.

"The trauma of someone screwing around inside your head or body, even if you really like the person, takes a while to process."

She encouraged me to keep writing and keep practicing gratitude. Later I will come to understand the post-traumatic stress would morph into something better. I call it my post traumatic spiritual growth, PTSG. Damn, I'm lucky.

The "other" Susan who is a published poet encourages my writing too. She had a dream about me before my emergency surgery. In her dream, I came out of the surgery more abled rather than less abled. Turns out, her dream came true. She always shows me the light.

Elisa is my unofficial doc as well as my friend. I gave her the password to the Mayo Clinic portal so she could read all the juicy medical reports. I'm sure we were not operating under HIPAA guidelines, but that's okay because we are governed by JIPAA, (that's the Jewish HIPAA where you tell everybody about all of your health issues, all the time.) She said she was grateful when Cameron finally put right my understanding of how the Ommaya reservoir implanted in my brain works because she did not want to have to correct me.

David is still my go-to rock. Once when Cameron and I stayed with him on a visit back to the Jersey shore, he said to Cameron,

"You better take care of her or I will need to come out to Arizona and kick your ass."

David is blown away by the impressive measures and ways Cameron takes care of me. A few weeks after surgery, I remember lying in bed and ugly-crying on the phone with David. I can still be comforted by his familiar, larger-than-life presence.

"I can't go through another brain surgery. I can't have a craniotomy. I can't do it."

"Jesus, darling, why are you always looking to borrow worry? Just enjoy your remarkable recovery happening right now. You know the drill, don't pull that trigger until you absolutely have to. We're not going to talk about this now. We can talk about it again in six months. Go. Enjoy your life. And tell Cameron I love him too."

After I tell Cameron that David sends his love, I thank him for not only being my rock, but for being my teacher in Watch and Wait. In my new wabi-sabi mindset, I realize that what I used to think of as Cameron's tendency to procrastinate on making decisions is another unexpected gift for me to learn from. Viewed through the prism of my new wabi-sabi perspective, it is also the perfection of WaWa. He watches and he waits so much better than I do. I want to follow his lead now instead of getting annoyed by what I used to label as procrastination. Gratitude has appeared in the place of irritation.

Greg and I have been through a lot together. We have shared the grief over losing his beloved wife and my dear friend Leslie who fought a long and hard battle with breast cancer, to the bitter end. She was the cancer patient and he was her caregiver. I think of both of them as strong warriors. I'm doing my adventure a bit differently, because I didn't personally relate to the warrior metaphor. Then I received an anonymous gift in the mail on my sixty-fourth birthday, a Rosie the Riveter Brain Tumor Warrior t-shirt. I tried it on and I too became a warrior. Thank you, Jenn.

Greg accepts me unconditionally in his own quiet way. One time he started to say something like, "Maybe someday we can talk about why you wouldn't consider doing another brain surgery if that's what might be needed."

"Because brain surgery is a roll of the dice."

Then I put up my defensive No More BS wall and he never brought the subject up again. Greg had his own medical adventures well before I stepped onto my path and understands about the trauma. Knowing how much he hates hospitals and seeing him show up to visit me in the Marvelous Mayo every day speaks volumes about our friendship.

CHAPTER 24: FAMILY OF ORIGIN CONVERSATIONS ON DEATH

We're OK with "This," Whatever the World to Come Looks Like

I'd never had planning discussions about end-of-life care with either of my parents, but their unique situations forced the conversation in our own unique family karmic way. Family provides me with some of the greatest teachers and I didn't have to look any further than my own DNA for lessons. It seems no matter what happened during our lifetimes, we looked to each other, in the end, to escort each other out. Weird how families of origin never seem to entirely lose their relevance, no matter how much we would like.

Arnold

My father wasn't around much. He is what psychologists call an "absent" father. One time he phoned me up, out of the blue, just after I had moved to Arizona for an experimental year to see if I might like desert living. I have no idea how he found my Phoenix phone number.

"Suze, it's Dad."

"Dad who?"

Chuckling is heard on both ends of the phone line.

"Got a favor to ask. I am going in for another quadruple bypass heart surgery next week. I need someone, a next of kin, willing and able to authorize pulling the plug at the first sign of me stroking out."

He wasn't worried about death, just morbidity. Losing control of mind and body. That's me too, especially now that I've been there and got miraculously rescued back.

Seriously, dude?! We hadn't spoken in years. This takes balls, even for him. But I am living in the Southwest now, so that would be cojones.

"Let me think about it."

He laughed again, this time in a way that made me feel we shared a camaraderie around the sheer chutzpah of his asking.

The next week, we met up in an Embassy Suites Hotel near John Muir Hospital. He showed me his pre-op instructions: a light evening meal and no food or drink after

10:00 pm. At dinner, I watched as he ordered and then devoured a 10-ounce steak, rare, smothered with sautéed onions and mushrooms, a side salad and garlic mashed potatoes. He washed it down with three extra dry vodka martinis and followed it up with a decadent flourless chocolate torte. After dinner, he left me to pay the bill and walked outside to smoke a few Marlboro cigarettes. I paid the bill on the credit card I was using to support myself for a year and we headed up to my hotel room. He slept on the couch. The next day, he came out of the surgery just fine. I flew back to Phoenix and never saw him again.

When he was actually dying for real, he was at his brother's house, staying with my Uncle Herb and Aunt Viv. They called me and said he really was dying this time and now would be the time to reconcile. In a panic, I called my brother and told him about our father's impending death. Michael said, "Ain't nothing to reconcile. We're good." I breathed a big sigh of relief. I showed up for my father with his fear of morbidity, he didn't need me in the face of his mortality.

Molly

My mother was always around. She is what psychologists call a "controlling" mother. Turns out reconciling anger and resentment with an absent father is a gazillion times easier and faster than being able to say, "we're good" with a controlling mother. I was used to the feeling of an absent father, so when death arrived, it wasn't all that different. It would take seven years after my mother's death and reconciling with two brain tumors first before I could truly say "we're good." When it finally happened, it appeared in the form of this senior adult coming of age memoir. Late bloomer, but better late than never.

One of the last conversations we had was about her final resting place. She had lost her voice by this time, but we were communicating with crystal clarity. My mother was always a planner. I think the planning may have given her a small sense of control in this uncontrollable world. She purchased her burial plot in a Jewish cemetery in Philadelphia many, many years before she died. I knew I would need to get her there.

As her time was drawing toward the end, I steeled myself with a triple shot venti latte from the Camp Verde

Starbucks and headed to the nursing home for "the talk." I was going to assert my needs and boundaries with her, and give her a chance to hear me speak. She was dying. This was something different between us. Even though I still felt like it was my job to protect and take care of her, it was the first time I was communicating with her as an adult with agency instead of the helpless child. She knew I was there for the talk.

First, I reassured her that I knew her wishes. Next, I made her a promise. "I will get you back to Philly."

She lay in her hospice bed, pale, thin and tired. I offered to pour some of my latte into a dixie cup for her, but she gave me a slight nod of her head, no. I took a long sip of caffeinated courage and a deep breath. I stalled. I got up and gave my dog Meka a dog biscuit. A few weeks earlier, my mom asked me to leave a box of dog biscuits in her room so she could treat Meka on our weekly visits. As I was leaving that day, she motioned me over to her and mouthed the words, "Take the dog biscuits."

"But I thought you wanted to keep them here in your room."

"They will be stale by the time you get back."

At the time, this line infuriated me. Today, more than seven years later, it cracks me up and I laugh out loud as I type it. She could be hilarious.

I steel myself for the death talk that we both know is coming. It's time. She asked me to take down the posed toothy smiling framed family portrait photographs of my brother's family that were displayed on her dresser top. My sister-in-law had prominently displayed them there on an earlier visit. I guess my mother didn't want them looking down or watching over her as she left this world. This was private. She was going out on her terms. Later, I would remove those photos from their frames, roll and tie them up like mini scrolls and place them inside the box containing my mother's ashes. The family she loved in her deeply flawed and very human way would accompany her on that leg of her journey.

"This is really hard for me, Mom." Then, I just blurted it out, the way she would have done. "I am wondering if you would be okay with cremation? You know I will get you back to Philadelphia, but it would be a lot easier if I could do it that way."

Cremation is not traditionally done in our Jewish religion.

Her facial expression was a familiar one. The disappointed face of my beaten down Jewish mother. I had seen it many times. Her voice was gone. She wasn't speaking, but her expression was still communicating, crystal clear. I began to interpret the familiar expressions and heard her voice. I wondered what happened to that sad but satisfied person that whispered in her best raspy but voiceless Frank Sinatra, "I did it my way" from her bed just a week or so before. I wanted that Molly back. Instead, I got the helpless but resigned victim.

"What can I do? You just go on and do what you need to do."

It was our coded language. I heard what she said and what she meant with this soft but sharp tone. I felt relief. She looked defeated. Gratitude was in short supply that day. I started to understand how having a plan can be a comfort and this one now gave me a small sense of control in my uncontrollable world.

It would take seven more years before I felt the most profound gratitude that my mother chose and honored me to be her companion, care and support on the final leg of her journey on this earth. Confronting death lays bare the spiritual core of our human condition. I didn't understand this at the time. All I felt was resentment that I had a difficult job to do.

The tote bag holding her cremains had the funeral home logo on the front. Walking through airport security together was surreal. I nervously handed the bag of cremains and the cremation certificate to the airport security staff. Molly had to be chemically tested to make sure she wasn't a bomb.

We arrived at our gate only to discover the flight to Philly had been canceled due to a weather microburst event there. Maybe this was my mother's last stand for being difficult. Maybe she wanted to show me one last time just how powerful she was and who was still in charge. Maybe she wanted to stay overnight in Arizona one more night and say goodbye to my brother. Maybe she just wanted to share one more bizarro laugh together.

Whatever the reason, it worked. We left the airport and went back to my brother's house. I placed her tote bag on their dining room table. I had made my peace with my

Mom, and was finding this last leg of our physical journey together pleasant and amusing. I didn't realize the surreal weirdness of it made my brother uncomfortable. Once I saw the discomfort on his face, I took her off his dining room table and carried her on my shoulder, tucked safely away in her blue canvas tote bag.

Molly and I flew out the next day. I cradled her cremains and held her tightly on my lap for the entire flight. She was sitting inside a small box, inside a royal blue tote bag with the funeral home logo facing outward. This would have pissed her off to no end, using her demise to advertise their business with what she would call words. She didn't like any kind of messaging to be advertised on clothing. She would not have approved of my brain tumor humor wear.

We eventually made it to the cemetery which was located in a noisy and congested Philadelphia suburb. We had a lovely graveside service. Her family showed up for her and gave her a proper Jewish ceremony. Years later, her beloved brother Henry would be buried next to her in the plot she originally intended for me or my brother. This makes me happy. Although my mother loved me and loved my brother deeply with all her heart and soul, the one and only person she truly trusted in this world was her beloved brother Henry. And now they could rest together, side by side, forever.

I naively hosted an early Mother's Day party in Molly's room. I didn't know it was also a goodbye party. My brother and his family came up from Phoenix. I bought two kinds of her favorite Entenmann's cake, lemon and raspberry. I served the cake on cute floral-patterned napkins with matching paper plates.

She was partly sitting up in bed, leaning on the wedge pillow I bought for her a few weeks before. Her eyes were proudly following Sophie, her first baby granddaughter, around the room. Sophie was being held almost as a protective shield by my brother. I understood. It was like my Pollyanna shield I would use in the posthumous tea party I held with Molly, in the ether.

When I offered her a plate with two small pieces of cake, she glared at me in a familiar way. I understood exactly what she was saying. "I said no more food or drink. Enough already with the morbidities."

Three weeks earlier, I heard Molly ask the hospice nurse how she could speed things up. The nurse told her matter-of-factly, "stop eating and drinking." And that is what she did. Her quality of life had finally overwhelmed her and she decided to tough it out and take leave. I hope when it is my time to go, I will have the grit and determination my mother showed to turn down a delicious piece of sweet Entenmann's coffee cake.

I made the sweet cake offering to her before I understood she had already made her choice to go. She had saved the most profound life lessons for last, but it would be a while before I understood them. I am still learning them. Her ripples carry on.

Alevasholem, Rest in Peace, Mom.

Michael

He is what a psychologist might call a wise older brother. The older we get, the closer we get. He has his own loving family and I know they have had "the talk" with each other about their mortality. Like his mother, he is a planner. Before my surgery, we talked about a plan to sign my paperwork like wills, advanced health and financial directives and powers of attorney. I knew he would have the ability to "pull the plug" at my first sign of stroke. Unlike my father, I didn't have the chutzpah to ask so directly.

Since Cameron and I aren't married, I needed to have legal paperwork to authorize someone else to make decisions for me if I couldn't make them myself. I thought it would be too difficult for Cameron to "pull the plug." Left to him, I'd be propped up in a lounge chair with a sweeping view of Mingus Mountain, with a dog and two cats on my lap, lapping up the soup dribbling down my chin. He would assure me everything was fine and tell me he loved me.

I knew Michael would have an easier time. Brain surgery is unlike any other surgery. Other kinds of surgeries have you wondering and hoping you're going to wake up. With brain surgery, you wonder if you're going to be there when you do wake up.

Under stressful situations, Michael takes control. I kept missing appointments to show up at his house with my paperwork so we could take it to his neighborhood UPS store and have it notarized. I knew he was getting impatient and annoyed with me, but my brain was foggy and I couldn't get it together to organize the paperwork. It was like my income taxes, whooshing over my head. I just couldn't seem to get it done.

One of my documents is called the *Five Wishes*. It is a plain language legal form put out by the hospice community. The format is personal rather than medical. It honors a more holistic perspective on end-of-life thoughts and that suits me just fine. We eventually got to the notary, one day before the surgery. While signing, I noticed his social security number is only one digit off from my mine. It made me realize how much we are connected, a shared life, at a deep DNA level.

Later, when it becomes clear I have come out of the surgery able to make my own decisions, he gets a little tougher with me. Like Bernie, he gets all up in my face while I am sitting in my hospital bed and says I need to take ownership of my tumors. I didn't even know what that meant. But, bro, did I ever follow through. I took it to the extreme. Not only have I taken ownership, I've given them names, identities and now I wear them as a badge of honor.

Later, in response to one of my bazillion kvetching emails about not wanting any more brain surgery but not wanting to let others down, he responded with one of his inimitable hard-core answers, advising me to channel our father. He says I am skilled in doing this. That confuses and hurts my feelings. Am I that selfish?

"Just drop the codependency and do whatever the fuck you want."

He advised me to fill out a "real" form and replace that woo-woo wishing on a star story with a legal advanced directive that explicitly spells out my desires. His directness can at times be jarring, but once I get over the initial jar, he usually influences my actions. He is our mother's son, after all. I love him and I know he loves me.

I filled out an application and register with a company called *Research for Life*, an Arizona based organ and tissue donor service. I wish to donate my whole body for medical education and disease research. It is a benefit to humanity, but it isn't just a selfless act of generosity. I admit that an equally compelling reason to donate my body to science with this organization is the sheer convenience of it.

There are no costs for cremation or for body transportation and they will even take you out on a boat ride and spread your ashes over the Pacific Ocean, if that is your choice. I tell Cameron where to find my laminated card, neatly tucked inside my wallet, behind the other laminated Medtronic card with the serial number and specifications of my Ommaya reservoir. All he needs to do is make the call for my ride pick up. I am not a natural planner, but it is comforting to have this plan in place too.

Morbidity

We used to mock my mother for her use of the word morbid, behind her back, of course. She complained how morbid it felt when my brother took his family to their annual summer beach vacation and didn't bring her along. She said it was morbid being left behind in Phoenix, alone. I remember rolling my eyes when she phoned me up to complain every July. I wanted to tell her she probably meant "morose," but she always liked a dramatic flair and did not like to be corrected.

Now I understand the word in its longer form and think about it all the time. In medical terms, morbidity is "any physical or psychological state considered to be outside the realm of normal well-being." Contrast that to mortality, "the state of being subject to death." If truth be told, I would take mortality—a spiritual death at home or in a quiet hospice setting—over the unknown morbidity effects of a brain tumor or brain surgery any day. Maybe that is because I already walked this walk of wet, wobbly, and wacky and I ain't about to go back there, to my worst fears. It is that less than living that I fear. Death is preferable.

Brain scans are a thing my mom and I have in common now. The last scan I accompanied her on was a fateful one. It was late in the afternoon on another hot day in Phoenix. Molly's neurologist at the Muhammed Ali Parkinson's Center was running two hours late. When we finally sat down with her, she shared Molly's scan results from the morning tests.

Everyone was tired. We were told and shown how Molly's brain was shrinking. When the neurologist shared this news with us, I watched Molly's whole body shrink down into her wheelchair, her large floral pattern purse taking up all the space on her tiny lap. She dropped her head into her hands and covered her eyes as if her shrinking brain needed the extra support of her hands. She didn't cry. She didn't speak. I sat there, silently witnessing, waiting for someone else to speak first.

On reflection, I believe hearing this news was the beginning of the end-of-life journey for my mother. She was more depressed than usual. She showed no animation. She wasn't losing her will to live, she was finding her will to die.

We left the neurologist's office and headed to the lobby, in silence. The medical transport van would be returning her to her nursing home. The silence didn't feel awkward. I was relieved to not have to talk. Then she finally broke it with a rhetorical question.

"So, what could be worse than your brain SHRINKING?"

This was my sad and defeated Jewish mother doing the asking. I had no answer that day. I said nothing. We just stared at each other. As usual, I was the first to look away from that pained glower on her face.

Fast forward seven years.

"Ask me that question again, Mom." Pinena and Pollyanna have an answer today. "What's worse you ask?

What if your brain was growing, not shrinking? As in brain tumors. Now that's morbidity. Can't top that one."

This is our variation on the Jewish one-upmanship of "You think you've got problems...." We call it tsuris, a Yiddish word for troubles.

Like mother, like daughter, not! We both have brain disease. I am using my disease to learn about gratitude and try to do better. My anger toward my mother recedes as my compassion for her illness grows. I forgive her. I appreciate how much she has given me. I understand now how she grew tired of watching and waiting for all of her shoes to drop. She said enough already with the morbidity.

I am learning how to watch and wait. I watch and wait for morbidity. I try to act with more self-control and less impulsivity. I see it leads to more feelings of self-respect. It is becoming a spiritual practice. As with any practice, it needs to be practiced. I am learning how to value this. I am not 100% there yet, but like the well-worn cliché, it is the journey, not the destination.

Until we are ready to embrace the mortality, how much morbidity is too much? Somewhere along the journey I made that vow. The one I plucked right off a favorite black hoodie with the ocean blue wave water graphic. "No More BS (brain surgery)."

I had no idea that this clever graphic would harden into an intractable core belief. Multiple brain surgeries are very common, especially for people with hydrocephalus. Cameron says, "You don't have hydrocephalus. You were cured with the ETV."

"Yeah, but I still have Pinena, the pineal tumor. And I am never going to ever have a craniotomy. I'm sorry, but I just don't have the strength or fortitude for it."

Cameron doesn't understand this way of thinking. I don't even like talking to him about it because I know it upsets him. I try to avoid the topic and mostly we do. Brain surgery is a crap shoot. Always. You never know what is there until you're on the inside. Even the most sophisticated MRI images can't tell a neurosurgeon how a tumor might stick to its host or how close you have to go to surrounding veins and structures. It's a risky gamble, even for the most brilliant and skilled hands and minds, like those of Bernie, my Kintsugi artist. One tiny nick or unexpected sneeze and whoopsie, there goes your personality, your movement and your independence.

My friend Noreen asks, "But no one has told you that you need another brain surgery, have they?"

No, they haven't. I just know it is always an option on the table. I am learning how to be calm and peaceful in my new normal Watch and Wait (WaWa) life, but it takes a lot of effort. I work on it through my imperfect-perfection wabi-sabi philosophy that I take with me everywhere I go. It's my own personal Zen koan. This is where I want to stay. I guess I need remedial reading on impermanence. And a lot more practice.

I understand that my tumors may grow, shrink, disappear or remain stable. And, their stable state can, like life, change at any time. Even an image in an MRI is a measurement just in the very moment it is captured. Brain tumor cells could very well go rogue as I step off the scan table. I may not show symptoms or know that until the next imaging.

Family karma

It is only now, through this writing, that I realize I shared the same fears my father had of "stroking out" and my mother's fears about her shrinking brain. I am afraid of becoming wet, wobbly and wacky again. Or worse. It's not about mortality or death. We all seem to be OK with that. It is about control, morbidity, and incapacitation. It's about our precious health and our human frailties.

My first (and hopefully last) brain surgery was wildly successful. Going back inside seems like Russian Roulette. Bernie is a brilliant brain surgeon and I trust him implicitly, but it's brain surgery. The kind of surgery where the air hits your brain and nothing is ever the same. You just never know how you will wake up.

CHAPTER 25: LIVING WABI-SABI
IN A WAWA WORLD

"In our instinctive attachments, our fear of change and our wish for certainty, we may undercut the impermanence which is our greatest strength, our most fundamental identity. Without impermanence, there is not process. The nature of life is change. All hope is based on process."
–Rachel Naomi Remen

"The waiting is the hardest part. Every day you see one more card. You take it on faith, you take it to the heart."
– Tom Petty

This is the final part of Act 3, where the paradoxical lessons of wabi-sabi calm me down. I don't feel the same kind of frenetic cerebral energy or need to chase down Buddhist principles of detachment or a single ancient Jewish text on which to hang all of my clothes. I understand and appreciate how my unique flaws, my brain tumors, have led me to my greatest strengths and treasures, a grateful outlook being the biggest treasure of all. I am continuously learning how to embrace impermanence of all things as the natural order and accept the good and inevitable pain of life with grace and gratitude.

I am grateful for the new wabi-sabi life I have been practicing and training myself in over the past year. If this is the new normal, then I'll take it. Learning to gratefully and gracefully accept the impermanence of all things in life. Nothing lasts forever and nothing is ever done.

Intuitively, I know there is a relationship between the uncontrolled inflammation of my autoimmune disease and my brain tumor, even if my brilliant neurodocs aren't interested in the connections. The immune system and the brain are still confusing to me. Are Pinena and Pollyanna viral in some way? I'm told no. Is there a connection between my chronically high inflammation numbers and the existence of the sisters? Maybe. Is it environmental? Probably, at least partially. It's all part of the not-so-cozy mystery. From all the research I've done over the years on the Ankylosing Spondylitis and my hyperactive immune system, the brain can be altered through inflammation. For now, I am choosing to stay focused on my excellent quality of life, accept the wisdom of not knowing and grateful to stay the course with the WaWa plan.

After a year of not performing, I am grateful the over-the-counter anti-inflammatory NSAIDs have started working again on my stiff and painful joints. I pray and trust that this continues and I won't need to take it to the next level of immune suppressant drugs. I am thankful my miracle ETV surgery is working and my cerebral spinal fluid flows. I pray, hope and trust that runaway inflammation doesn't run roughshod through the blood-brain barrier, even though I still don't understand the science and the beauty of how that even works. Imperfect perfection, for now. Wabi-Sabi.

We plan and G-d laughs. – *Yiddish proverb*

April, 2020; A letter to my beloved neurodocs (who are also my spiritual teachers)

To My Dearest Neurodocs:

Thinking of you and hoping you are all healthy and safe! I feel such an abiding kinship with you and worry about you out there on the front lines of Covid-19. I am scheduled for an MRI on May 4 and follow-up appointment with Dr. Porter on May 5 (Cinco de Mayo Clinic, pandemic-style).

I am expecting a call from Mayo to reschedule, as it's now a routine scan and probably not worth the risk of virus exposure. We are spending this pandemic time at home, and I am writing a memoir. I've had almost a year to work on strategies around fears and uncertainty of my personal health crisis that the world is now grappling with on a global level with the Covid-19 virus. It's impossible to not see the bizarre parallels.

I've been given lots of great gifts in my life, but none rarer or more precious than the ETV surgery. Not every gift comes wrapped up with a bow. But life sometimes wraps up her gifts as metaphors, in little bows for us, exactly when we need them. I don't always recognize life's wisdom when it is given. In addition to world-class medical treatment, each one of you has given me a profound spiritual gift. The recognition of this would take time to understand.

In my pre-surgery neuro assessment with Dr. Porter, I asked if I could use a pen and paper for the math problems or look at my phone's calendar to figure out the date. The answer was no. I was sad and angry. And now I see the beautiful wisdom in that answer no. Best to look at reality with open eyes and discomfort so we can see what needs fixing.

I wanted so badly to thank you when I saw your face after waking up from surgery, Dr. Patra, but I couldn't stop sobbing long enough to speak. Later, you quietly explained the sloshing sound in my head and reassured me, "'twill resolve." This answer has become our family spiritual mantra.

After surgery, when Dr. Bendok pointed a finger at me, just like a Zen master, and said two words, "You're better!" and walked out, I got the spiritual lesson of getting a second chance at life and understanding I can now do better too!

So, I will sit in my WaWa (Watch and Wait) spiritual practice, morphed from my treatment plan, and try to relax as I wait for the Mayo cancellation call. I hope you are staying healthy and safe and am looking forward to the time when you think it is best for me to visit. And I look forward to being able to bring you a box of See's gratitude chocolate once again!

In gratitude and love,

Susan

May, 2020 – Scanxiety Visit #4

The Mayo Clinic cancellation call never came. My scan was not being postponed. So, I can drop the whole "spiritually developed" mask and swap it out for a surgical one. I pack up my mask and place it inside my old and well-worn portmanteau for the journey – Scanxiety.

It is different this time. There is a strange quiet but intense energy inside a hospital in a Covid-19 pandemic. It is difficult to explain, but there is a tension you can feel.

Cameron and Paisley wait outside in the parking lot. No visitors allowed inside the hospital today. My temperature is taken as I enter the building and I exchange my beautiful blue cloth mask, hand-made by Cameron's sister Joanne, for a pleated surgical one. My writer buddy Nancy commented on the pre-tube ride photo I sent from outside the Mayo building. She was impressed with how my hand-made blue-cloth mask matched my outfit.

"I had not figured you for a fashionista."

Even though I knew there was a threat of an invisible lurking virus, the hospital still seemed like a safe place. Today, the MRI was a no-frills ride. I have never seen the waiting room so empty. My temperature was taken again and six Covid-19 screening questions were asked. Ironically, we were asked more Covid-19 screening questions last week when we had to call for a AAA tow truck for our forty-five-year-old classic car breakdown.

I was planning to ask for the oldies soundtrack for the MRI, aka The Tube ride, but there was no music offered today. I was picked up about thirty seconds after my cannula IV was inserted and dangled from my forearm, ready for the shot of the dreaded Gadolinium contrast that "enhances" the tumors. I didn't even have time to send out a snarky text to Cameron as I usually do from the inner sanctum tube ride waiting room. No waiting today.

The techs and I had a short chat about my Ommaya reservoir. I had to return to the locker to retrieve my laminated Medtronic card to show them the serial number and the specs. This required another disinfectant wipe down of the locker keys, another swiping under the hands-free Purell sanitizer wall dispenser and an escort back to the big magnet room. The hospital staff are taking virus precautions very seriously and the stress is showing on their faces. You can see it in their eyes, under their masks. We walked past a medical scale.

"Oh, can I just hop on the scale for quick sec?" I wanted to see if I had gained back any weight since my last weigh in. The nurse looked at me with a somewhat shocked and disgusted expression, as if to say, *Seriously?*

I apologized, acknowledging it was a frivolous idea and jumped in line to head back to the tube, forearm throbbing from the tightly taped cannula, ready for the light-me-up juice shot. No frills today.

I didn't realize until I was being pushed in that I would be wearing the mask inside the tube. Whoa, good thing I am not claustrophobic. I decided to treat it as an applied mindfulness exercise Jon Kabat Zinn talks about in his teachings. About thirty-five minutes into the ride, while trying to stay focused on my breath, my concentration was interrupted by an unexplained whole-body sweating episode. I am well past my time for hot flashes.

I decided to add a bit of Jewish prayer this time to the mindfulness practice. Try and sharpen the focus. Breathe in, one, two, three four. *Baruch.* Hold, one, two, three, four. Breathe out the fear and tension, one, two, three, four, *Hashem.* Hold, one, two, three, four. Notice how the accordion surgical mask moves in and out with the breath.

Notice the moistness all over the body from the profuse sweat coming out of every pore. Next came the affirmations. Breathe in, equanimity. Hold. Exhale, gratitude.

I was in another zone when the nurse pulled me out for the Gadolinium contrast. He told me not to move my head and complimented me on how well I was doing at keeping perfectly still. And then it was over.

I had a bit of trouble sitting up, felt slightly dizzy but hugely relieved. I was reminded to drink loads of fluids to flush out the contrast over the next day. I was escorted to my locker and dressing room, and a tag was placed on the door as a reminder to the staff for another wipe down. As I was being escorted back to the lobby, I decided to ask a question I knew could not be answered.

"Did you see my tumor, Nurse Amy?"

She pointed to her name badge and said, "I have many credentials after my name, but MD is not one of them."

Today was all about high efficiency, all business and no frills. In and out.

There will be no family ritual gathering at Chompie's Jewish Delicatessen on this trip. We are in the midst of a

Covid-19 pandemic in a Republican state. There will be no visiting or overnight stay with Greg. No shopping for See's gratitude chocolates for the neurodocs and no visits for Cameron to Zia Records. There will only be gratitude for whatever is next.

The next day, we set up at home, in the living room, for the telemedicine meeting with Dr. Porter on Zoom. Last week I wrote a piece on attending my friend's father's Zoom funeral. This meeting would be equally as strange, looking at images of my brain, in all its tumored glory, on a Zoom meeting screen. I have attended many Zoom meetings, but this was Cameron's first. He helps me set up all the technical stuff, all the time, so he knows exactly how it works.

Dr. Porter looks gorgeous on screen in her crisp white doctor coat. She begins with two words, "thrilled" and "pleased" and that, in turn, made me feel thrilled and pleased. The video quality from the Mayo Clinic is excellent. As always, she doesn't waste any time.

"Your scans look good."

Cameron and I both breathe big audible sighs of relief. Dr. Porter complimented me again on my writing and we chatted a bit about how we were all coping in the new world disorder of Covid-19. She is home-schooling her kids and of course juggling a busy full-time neuro-oncology schedule. She talked about her gratitude for the Mayo being well resourced. I am grateful too.

She started sharing her screen with images of my brain from three months ago, side by side with the images from the most recent one. It looked like a mirror, with Pinena sitting in dead center on both sides. At first look I said,

"Oh, hello my lovely butterflies!" These days, it warms my heart to see Pinena and Pollyanna quietly bathing in my free-flowing cerebral spinal fluid.

Dr. Porter manipulated the views to show us different angles of my brain, but I had already checked out and was celebrating the bottom line: stable. I did not need to see stable at every angle. One word was good enough for me. Of course, we will pore over every single technical word once the radiology report gets posted to the portal. For today, the word stable brings tears to my eyes and is enough.

I will now spread out the scans from quarterly to every four months and possibly then move it out to every six months if Pinena continues to quietly age and peacefully calcify in place, deep inside my brain.

Baruch Hashem. Thanks to G-d. And thanks, always, to Bernie. I still believe in G-d and I still believe in science.

My WaWa (Watch and Wait) spiritual path and treatment plan continues, but the memoir period is coming to a close. I am ready to embark on the next chapter as I grow into my WaWa life.

If I never set foot inside a Jersey Shore WaWa convenience store again, I will always be a Jersey Girl. I hope to have "pleasing" and "thrilling" stable scans with "grossly unremarkable" tumors forever. I will always be grateful to be on my lifelong WaWa spiritual journey. Pinena and Pollyanna remain with me as my symbiotic reminders about how life can always change on a dime and to always live gratefully. This moment, this breath, this word is all we are promised.

The not-so-cozy mystery continues.

This is not the end.

"Life is movement from mystery to mystery. Mystery has the power to comfort, offer hope, and lend meaning."
– Rachel Naomi Remen

"It is only through mystery and madness that the soul is revealed."
– Thomas Moore

EPILOGUE
THERE BUT FOR THE GRACE OF G-D GO I

Reading neurosurgeon Henry Marsh's memoir *Do No Harm* was powerful. Then sitting down with Cameron to watch *The English Surgeon*, the documentary based on the book, was emotionally hard-hitting. Tears were streaming down my face through the entire film, and not only the scenes filming the actual surgery, when I had to leave the room. Henry Marsh is a British neurosurgeon who regularly shares his surgical skills, talents and time, treating poor and desperate brain tumor patients in Ukraine, free of charge. We watched this film about nine months into the healing journey because we thought we wanted to understand what it was like from Bernie's perspective. We couldn't imagine how he could do this work day in and day out.

The poor hospital environment in Ukraine is without modern neurosurgery equipment and tumors are often found only after it is too late for treatment. Throughout the film, Henry Marsh makes difficult medical and ethical decisions, balancing risks and possible benefits, just like my world-class neurodocs do, but without the benefit of the world-class equipment, facilities and resources that I am privileged to receive.

I've come to see how our family, personal, cultural, emotional and even ancestral histories impact trauma healing. My ancestors came from Jewish ghettos and fled the pogroms in Russia and Ukraine, with no money, no English, speaking only their native Yiddish language. It is impossible not to think, *there but for the grace of G-d go I.*

When Cameron and I sat down to watch the film, we wanted to understand our crazy adventure from our neurosurgeon, Bernie's perspective. But it ended up going so much deeper for me. The impact felt like it was happening at a soul level. It is as Henry Miller said, "*One's destination is never a place, but a new way of* seeing." I see my trauma and my healing in new and different ways.

I am grateful.

GLOSSARY

Benign [banin] adj. gentle and kindly. In disease, generally not harmful in effect. In brain tumors, even "benign" tumors of the brain can kill. In general, tumors with benign histology do not turn into malignant ones, but for brain tumors the distinction is not clear and there is a continuum of behavior of brain tumors.

My brain tumor Pinena is likely benign, but that doesn't mean she is always benevolent.

Endoscopic Third Ventriculostomy ETV: surgical procedure for treatment of hydrocephalus in which a talented and brilliant neurosurgeon creates an opening in the floor of the brain's third ventricle through a burr hole. This allows the cerebrospinal fluid to flow, bypassing the obstruction called Pinena.

My ETV was so wildly successful, it cured my wet, wobbly and wacky symptoms entirely.

Muse {myooz} (n) (In Greek and Roman mythology) each of the nine G-ddesses, the daughters of Zeus and Mnemosyne, who preside over the arts and sciences. A person or personified force who is the source of inspiration for a creative artist.

Pinena and Pollyanna are my muses and serve as co-authors of this memoir.

Pineal gland: A small, pine-coned shape endocrine gland located between the two hemispheres, deep in the center of the brain.

The mystics call the pineal gland a "third eye," source of intuition and once thought to be where the soul is located.

Portmanteau: (n) a made-up word blending the sounds and combining the meaning of two other words.

I am setting my intention and swapping out my portmanteaus, from scanxiety to scantastic.

Scanxiety: (n) Anxiety and worry that accompanies the period of time leading up to an MRI and the time between undergoing the scan and receiving the results.

The scanxiety she felt as she awaited the results of her brain MRI felt akin to putting her head back on the chopping block.

Schwannoma tumor: A common benign intracranial growth of rogue cells.

"Oh, that's just a little schwannoma, nothing to worry about, dear."

Symbiotic (adjective): involving interaction between two different organisms living in close physical association. Denotes a mutually beneficial relationship between different people or groups.

The brain tumors are nourished by the Jersey Girl's blood and they provide her with the creative impetus to write her story.

Tsuris: (n) Yiddish. Aggravating troubles.

Oy, it gives me such tsuris when you won't pick up the phone and call me.

Wabi-Sabi: (n) The beauty in the imperfect, impermanent and incomplete.

Today my brain is hosting two wabi-sabi tumors, named Pinena and Pollyanna, in a perfectly imperfect symbiotic relationship.

Watch and Wait (WaWa): A disease treatment protocol where time is allowed to pass before medical intervention or therapy is used, withholding treatment until measurable parameters change or symptoms appear.

My WaWa treatment began as a medical protocol and ended up morphing into a spiritual practice.

Zen koan: (n) a paradox to be meditated upon, used to train Zen Buddhist monks to abandon ultimate dependence on reason and to force them into gaining intuitive enlightenment.

In a brain tumor diagnosis or a coronavirus pandemic's limbo, the only thing certain is more uncertainty.

ACKNOWLEDGMENTS

This is an entire book of acknowledgements. When I finished writing, I wanted to rewrite it and call it Thank-You Letters from a Grateful Brain Tumor Survivor. I know it sounds cliché, but without all the beautiful people in my life and in this book, I literally would not be here now, able to write these words.

A special thanks and debt of gratitude to my coach and editor, Susanne Dunlap. When I expressed this desire to "start over," her wise words of wisdom kept me moving forward. She said it is tempting to think how I could make this better or write it in a cleverer way, but at some point, you simply have to let go and declare it finished. She says everything can be better or different, but done is sometimes best of all. Once she told me, with just a bit of irony, Pinena was being redundant. I wish. She is a patient and wise teacher. I am grateful to have met her on this incredible journey.

Thank you, Alyson Sheldrake, my first beta reader and friend, whose "how hard can it be?" attitude inspired me at every step of the project.

Thank you, Linda Cardillo and Bellastoria Press for allowing me to share my story, even as I am still reluctant to do so, still wondering if "it's good enough" and for telling me you recognized my voice from my writing when we first spoke on the phone.

Thank you to Chelsey Clammer and the Women on Writing (WOW) program where I had the good fortune to participate in your Writing from the Body course. And thank you to all the talented and generous writers whose paths have crossed mine and who never even blinked a "that's weird" eye when I introduced them to my girls, Pinena and Pollyanna.

A big thank you to artists and sisters Teegan and Jade from Printee Line Drawings https://www.printee-prints.co.uk/ for my cover art. Their designs reflect their love for minimalism and every one of their designs is created to tell a story. When I purchased my Pinena and Pollyanna line art from these talented artists, half of the proceeds were donated to The Brain Tumour Charity, based in the UK. https://www.thebraintumourcharity.org/get-involved/donate/

I will be donating any proceeds from this book to the Mayo Clinic brain research. I am paying it back. Contributing to research that helps save lives is a very meaningful way to also pay it forward. If you are moved to share support, here are a few ways to do it.

Mayo Clinic has three ways to make a gift:

1) **By Mail**: Please indicate when sending the gift that it is to be designated in support of "Brain Cancer Research." Checks can be made out directly to "*Mayo Clinic*" and sent to: Mayo Clinic, Department of Development, 200 First St SW, Rochester, MN 55905.

2) **By Phone**: To make a gift by credit card or to speak to a Development Representative, please call 507-284-2264 or 855-852-8129 (toll-free) between 8 a.m. and 5 p.m. CST, Monday through Friday. Please indicate to the Development Representative that the gift is to be designated in support of "Brain Cancer Research."

3) **Online:** Gifts can be made with a credit card online by visiting https://philanthropy.mayoclinic.org/donateMC. Where you are asked to select a designation for your gift,

simply select "Other" and type in "Brain Cancer Research" when you see the text box appear. Your automatically-generated email receipt will not specify your "Other" designation, but we will see it on our end and process it accordingly.

Here are three more charities involved in brain tumor research and support.

Hydrocephalus Association: https://www.hydroassoc.org/ All checks made payable to the Hydrocephalus Association can be mailed to: 4340 East West Highway, Suite 905, ATTN: Carrie Miller, Donor Relations Manager, Bethesda, MD 20814. Please note that the gift is to be designated in support of "Research" on behalf of Susan Spector.

The American Brain Tumor Association:
https://www.abta.org/

National Brain Tumor Society: https://braintumor.org/

CPSIA information can be obtained
at www.ICGtesting.com
Printed in the USA
BVHW071543090321
602013BV00005B/998